THE *art* OF YOUR
ENERGY II:
THE GODSPHERE

MARI BECKMAN

THE ART OF YOUR ENERGY II: THE GODSPHERE
By Mari Beckman

Published by
Doce Blant Publishing, North Port, Florida 34291
www.doceblantpublishing.com

Cover by Thomas Beckman
Interior Design by The Deliberate Page

Paperback ISBN: 978-1955413251
Spiral ISBN: 978-1955413268
ePub ISBN: 978-1955413282

Library of Congress Control Number 9781955413251

Printed in the United States of America

www.doceblant.com

Table of Contents

CHAPTER 1

What's New?

"The first book was finished, but the project has just begun." ~ ***Saint Francis of Assisi***

My first book, *The Art of Your Energy, Galactic and Celestial Light Codes for Healing* and Empowerment was published in the late summer of 2021. Soon afterward, I began to write this book, *The Godsphere*.

The AOYE codes are divided into three books. The original 33 codes hold the template of their own unique system made up of Galactic and Celestial wisdom and power. The living codes are born from the quantum field containing scalar (nature) energy guided by Nikola Tesla, and are held within my energetic field. The codes are held by Archangel Metatron, Archangel Sandalphon, the Arcturians and Ascended Master Kuthumi. This book presents the next codes, 34-68.

Why Do the Codes Work the Way They Do?

The first 33 codes were designed to ease the human, animal, land, or structure into an open state of healing, regeneration and empowerment. Why does it work? The codes balance your energy in zero point (or infinite source) with your own heart and the Sun. The codes are a spark or ignition to open up. It's a very simple modality, reiki-like, and it also can be used as a divination tool to find out more about yourself and others. A few codes have an association with an archangel or being of light. There are also codes inspired by special people in my life.

I teach classes on The Art of Your Energy modality so that anyone can learn how the codes work and how to use the system. The codes are added to the student's energy field during the final class and then can be used by the healer as their own modality.

This book is a workbook for the classes and a book that explains my ongoing journey as a shaman and channel. My hope is that people are inspired to listen closely to the natural world and their guides.

But wait! There's more!

The Skills

During 2022, I began to realize that there are skills associated with certain codes. The Ladder, Lock and Key and Offset, and code combinations classes were then developed.

The Ladder is a code, a skill, and a spiritual tool. Using the code, the Ladder releases you from the place where you became stuck on your path. I first employ the code, then use the Ladder to clairvoyantly view information about the client I am reading. Depending on where they stand on the Ladder, I can tell quite a bit about that person.

The code called, "Universal Lock and Key" came about in response to the question I asked of my guides, "Why don't some people heal?" The answer was a new code and skill. It began with the understanding of a lock, a key, a door, and a house. I work closely with my guidance team and my highest self to receive information in divine timing, or sometimes I receive everything all at once. When something comes in all at once, my guides call that "central processing."

The key is the thought, the lock is the emotion, and the door and house are symbols for zero point. The skill provides ten options to find and clear the seeker's unique sticking point with its own key called, "The Offset."

The zero point code (#5 from book 1) was created to contain the infinity symbol (lemniscate) or Uraeus. This code is held by Archangel Michael of the Sun. The zero point field is where we come into balance. My symbol for the zero-point field is a selenite singing bowl. In addition, I received platforms, columns, and skills that came through all at once; where work can be done in higher dimensions.

*The code Universal Lock and Key with Offset is a precision tool to clear the blockages that were put up in a trauma state. ~ **Nikola Tesla***

In the first book, the first 33 codes have very simple graphics. All the codes hold the energy that is infused by the Sun. In this second book, the codes have taken on more sacred geometry and colors as the work has evolved. There are now enough symbols and information for book 3. Some of the symbols show human avatar figures. I named them "Bob" and "Belynda" after special people in my life.

Once the original codes came out of me, I knew all at once how to use them and then I had to learn to work with their energy! The longer I work with the codes, the more I understand what they can do as we evolve. Children love them! Pets understand them, and the environment accepts them easily.

I channeled all of the information with the help of my guides I call the Team of Light and the Holy Ones. I practiced coding with friends and then I had to learn to flow the codes out into a large group. My gratitude goes out to my private Facebook group, Hands of Light, for trying out the original codes when I offered them early on. This group sends out prayers and healing for people who ask for it.

The AOYE coding method is taught in a class setting or remotely online. I humbly thank my students for helping me to better understand these remarkable codes and for trusting me to teach them the system.

How to Use This Manual

The words channeled throughout the book from my Team of Light and Holy Ones will raise your vibration as you read the stories, meditations, journeys, and decrees. My team of light chose where their words appear in this book. They tell me the book is like a journey with signs and information along the pathway. As the Masters speak, feel their words in your heart and if the frequency resonates, you will know that they are speaking to you. Occasionally, the message was personal to me. Mostly, the Masters were explaining a concept or lesson for everyone. This manual contains the images of the codes that can be added, Reiki-like, to your energetic system. My hope is that you will begin to experience your own light codes that flow into you. As we become more sensitive, we will recognize that each person is able to feel and understand codes and frequency upgrades and use them for health and expansion.

Many of us were considered the "black sheep" in our biological family, the nomad in our monad, so to speak! So, I tell my story, along with the words of our guides and guardians, because I know every spiritual person has felt lonely, and felt as if they stick out like a purple thumb! If you are alone, find your soul family. I am grateful for mine!

I am a shaman, and the shaman's journey is non-linear. Some events in this book are not in chronological order. These events happened as I wrote this book, and at the same time, the shamanic path spiritually opened me further. The stories represent how the messages came to me and my expanding awareness. My journey looked this way, yours will look different. I travelled physically, but your journey can happen around the fire in your backyard. As the codes came in, I began to heal in layers. I have chosen to tell my story here in the hope that you may see that we all have the ability to do this, to heal, and live a sacred life.

Art of Your Energy Classes

I am the keyholder of the codes and teach classes demonstrating the use of the codes and techniques as specified in AOYE skill classes. Once you have the codes within you, they are yours forever and can be used daily and sent to others. You are also able to teach the class by using the manual with your own students.

The codes are passed by boosting them energetically into the body of a client or student in a specific process. This powerful modality is easily understood and a lot of fun. Each code has a group name, its own name and a number. Don't worry if you cannot visualize; this healing happens with intention through your higher self. The codes are gentle but powerful and work on the mind, body and emotions, as well as with the spirit. I humbly ask that the codes are used as drawn, along with the information on how to generate the system taught in the AOYE I class.

When it comes to clearing a building, the codes will work to clear impacted emotions and chaos and bring movement to stuck energy. I have used them successfully on land, water, plants and trees.

Use the codes joyfully, as they are given to you in the same spirit. Joy shall come if joy is anticipated.
~ Ascended Master, Jesus Christ

Art of Your Energy Reiki

The first five codes of the original 33 are also Reiki symbols. I had no idea that these five codes worked in this way until I understood, through my guides, that there was to be an Art of Your Energy Reiki class. On April 3, 2022, the first Art of Your Energy Reiki Class was given, and the 5 codes were used for the very first time as Reiki symbols.

I saw the golden river in a vision in 2021. This river is a stage prior to the rainbow bridge and open to me during visions of assisting souls to cross over to the other side. As a clairvoyant, these symbols come to me so that I can understand the stages of a soul's passing.

In my vision, I was led through a downy, yellow light to an energetic platform. I could see animals of all types. Passing by me were elephants, bears, deer, wolves, dogs, and cats and so many other animals. Birds too! This river flowed as far as I could see. As a psychopomp, I gave my word to always assist animals or people that are trapped at any stage on the way home. Sometimes certain souls need help to cross over.

Then I saw the rainbow bridge! This bridge was made of every color of light from this world and beyond. I saw pets that I recognized as my own and even some, I knew, belonged to other people. People, too, were walking forward at the same time to begin their journey back home.

This vision was part of my master initiation to Art of Your Energy Reiki. Goddesses carrying the frequency of the Maiden, Mother and Crone came to me at the same time. They taught me that meeting them at the crossroads was part of the next step to teach Reiki. I was given a blessing and the energetic upgrade needed to teach this class.

This type of Reiki ignition, (called a boost in AOYE Reiki) unites us through the star tribes. A group I am part of called, "The Small Group" watched the tribes come together in a vision in the summer of 2023. There will be more about this ceremony in Chapter 11.

The uniting of all tribes has occurred. As above, so below. Your sacred geometry tells a story. Walk through the Stargate into the columns of golden light as you are home on New Earth. Give thanks today as the ancestors all do. ~ ***Reverend Dr. Martin Luther King***

There are many types of Reiki available now. If Reiki is a modality of healing that calls to you, find the lineage and teacher that you resonate with. Some healers choose to walk the original path, and some have branched off to create their own lineage. The groups that are newly created are woven into a vast system of older energies and practices.

No matter the lineage, the links we forge with other souls in healing groups or classes will be an enduring connection of light upon light. Imagine this connection is a soft, landing place made of golden threads; a blanket tossed to heaven and then floating easily into your arms.

Go forth as you are shown. May God bless you all without worry or concern for the past. ~ ***Master Usui: Original Reiki***

The Tenets or Main Principles We Hold in *The Art of Your Energy* Reiki

1. We serve in power, not force

2. We grow as we walk forward

3. We witness and observe

4. We speak up for others and ourselves

5. We are at once the student and the teacher

6. We hold our frequency in peace and ease

7. We hold our grid point in celebration

8. We love, and we are love

9. We care for our vessel tenderly and with reverence

10. We hold animals and all nature in the highest esteem. From the ant to the great Sequoia, all are equal and of value

The Four Directions

The Golden Columns of Light, the Stargate, the Violet Flame, and the Blue Column of Light establish the four directions in any work we do in the Art of Your Energy modality. These four directions hold divine space and energetic safety when work is being done. The AOYE system is balanced by Star and Stone. The golden columns are symbols for Archangel Metatron. The Selenite Path and Golden Overlay are symbols for Archangel Sandalphon.

My Guides describe the Four Directions below:

*The octahedron and the Golden Columns of Light shall establish the Stargate. The Stargate aligns with Sirius star. Welcome to the next level of Art of Your Energy. ~ **Commander Ashtar***

*The pink light of the Stargate supports all in love. True creativity can flow in its resonance, the heart and mind entrain in its frequency. The Stargate gently pushes all forward, all by way of a peaceful motion. ~ **Holy Mother Mary, Universal Angel***

*The Violet Flame is the motivator in zero point. Let the light do its job for humanity. ~ **St Germain***

*Turn on the power in your human vessel by calling in the Golden Column of Light. The Blue Light Column grounds and rises at the same time. ~ **Seraphim Angel, Seraphiel***

*When the four directions are called forth, protection, creativity and the power of forward energy are created. This is the niri ma kasu, or The Godsphere. One's energy rises in the Stargate. You stand in a place of acceptance to heal and release. The Blue Light Column both grounds and assists you to rise up into a higher frequency. I am grateful to be here with all of you as the New Golden Age unfolds. I welcome you to this next book of codes and teaching from the voices of the Masters and the Holy Ones. Please join me and be on the lookout for new beginnings everywhere! ~ **Nikola Tesla***

The Godsphere

In the fall of 2021, I traveled to four cities to take a small break. I was guided to stay with friends and ground, channel, write, and "have fun," or so the guides said. My team asked me "to be close to those who love you, and if you are appreciative and grateful, you shall take home a ready project."

The guidance came to be 100% true and not only did I organize this book, but I met several new guides that you will hear from in this book.

Another Step Towards Healing, The Pod

During the trip I was fortunate to have a healing session with artist and healer Jeffery Azanon St. Rose and his energetic device called, the "Elven Chamber." The Elven Chamber is a dimensional meditation device based on his amulet, The Elven Cocoon of Light. It is about nine feet long, and quite tall. The Pod opens like a comfortable nest. I climbed inside.

Spirit told me that this healing with Jeff would clear blockages due to the lack of love early in this lifetime. It would assist the opening of my soul mastery language. As this blockage of lack cleared, abundance would flow in all directions.

When I was in the Elven pod, I felt many beings with hands upon my body; an Orion, an Arcturian and more! Jeff does his work outside the pod and does not touch the client. I felt a crown was removed and replaced. I believed I was awake and completely aware.

I saw an elemental lifetime that I had not been aware of and saw several friends as elemental beings in a vision while in the Pod.

We have lived so many lifetimes, and in many realms, but in this lifetime seeing the fairy aspect of myself was a big surprise! I felt myself fly up and then land again on the ground and I noticed the layers of leaves and mycelium, soil and decaying plant matter. I saw a giant foot come down over me, ending my life.

Below are the words of more of the beings I met that day.

*Well done to place yourself in the mighty hands of our brother. You need support to grow now. You need to rest. This trip contains more surprises. ~ **The Sasquatch, Elder Brother***

We observed a master and student today. This is a very typical way for us to interact when healing is taking place. We observe and assist in the portal. Time holders, you could call us. We hold space, literally.

Your healing was just and well done. Your vessel received it well. The pain overall shall retreat as you work through your systems and higher bodies. At this moment the mental body continues to get this type of healing. Three more are needed. We are Sun beings, a reflection of you. ~ **The Golden Spoon, Galactic Being from The Sun:**

During my second trip up North to visit Jeff and the pod, I took my friend Angela. She told me that I snored through the entire session! My mind must have needed the rest as much as the rest of me did. I occasionally fall asleep during journey classes that I sit in, and my own students do, as well. Not to worry, the work still gets done.

Energy Update from Summer 2023

The energy upon planet Earth is now such that many more types of elementals and other realms can be seen. They have always been living with us on Earth. We are just now able to hold a higher light of ourselves and can see what has always been here. The Avian realm, the Small World of bugs and insects and the trees speak to those who have ears to hear. I believe we all have become more sensitive and empathic.

You can see the new colors and the beings that are coming in clearly as they show themselves to the eyes of the world now. This is my message to you and anyone who seeks us for peace. You cannot miss the frequency of peace on this glorious new morning full of possibilities! Just look around you! The colors are more vibrant, the Sun is brighter. If you cannot see this out of your window, then look inside yourself. The true mirror of peace starts with you. Planet Earth and animals are already in the higher dimensions. What are you waiting for? Are you ready to begin? ~ **Holy Mother Mary, Universal Angel**

'Disclosure' is laughable, really, in the way that most think about it. All that is needed is to look up and outside with an open mind. Your physical body feels our ships. More and more citizens of the planet are remembering who they are. Pull the energy of the Sun along with love into your own hearts. In the near future, other things will take importance over money and material goods for more and more citizens of the Earth. ~ **Commander Ashtar**

The Stargate

On this day, after the healing in the pod, I was able to understand that the pink pyramids I had been bringing onto the earth were stargates, portals to a healing realm. I was able to open one on my friend's property. At that moment new codes came through. The new codes come only when they are in divine timing. When my friends returned home from their trip, I let them know I had opened that stargate on their property. They said they could feel it! "Leave it, we love it!' they said.

The Stargate aligns with Sirius, our home, and spiritual sun. Sirius is two times larger than Earth and twenty-six times brighter than the Sun. Use the Stargate well. ~ **Commander Ashtar**

CHAPTER 2

Time and Timing, the Rise and Fall of Your Frequency

During the Spring Equinox of 2023, I wrote in my journal about the Aquarian times ahead. The new moon energy of that month felt like we were going where we'd never been before...here on this planet, anyway!

That old energy, like a drawn back bow, was completely gone and the arrow now had begun to fly true. It was a blissful moment to know that we were about to see the dawning of actualized human potential.

I find that it is useful to check in daily and keep a journal of what I see, hear and feel. I often receive messages, from my guides and higher self, regarding the things I observe. Then later, I go back and celebrate what has come to pass.

*It is nigh time to consider this prison called 'time'. People worry and fret and spend time worrying about having enough of it! You get anxious about how much time a certain task takes to complete. How much time does it take to arrive where you want to go? I am here to tell you it takes what it takes. And if that is all you need to know, then you are free. From my heart, I tell you, spending time on yourself is the greatest investment you'll ever make. ~ **Benjamin Franklin:***

So, why do we stay stuck until the moment in timing when the seals pop and you move forward? We have always done it this way and we want to be right!

- We want someone else to be wrong.

- We have a dog in the fight!

- Those around us think a certain way and we don't wish to stand out as different or "other."

- We're running an old unconscious program.

When Someone Projects onto You

Ask yourself, what part did I play? Can we work this out? Ask yourself if they are committed to a belief and may not be ready to hear you. The next step is to prove your point or step aside. Give it time if the relationship is important to you. We are learning to be better listeners. When someone only listens long enough to take over and make their point, we feel unheard.

Perhaps it's time for our truth to come out front and center.

*When Star and Stone align, there is freedom. This belief is held by many now upon the Earth. Each soul has a job to do. More shall realize this as the trappings of modern life become repellent and seen as the truth versus the lies that have been told or uncovered. Really, what does each soul need to be happy? The answer is very little. ~ **Grandfather Rainbow, Medicine Man, Puyallup and Tulalip, Washington State***

Ascension and Ascension Symptoms

These channeled messages remind us to think of the bigger picture when noticing our bodies and surroundings reflect the feeling of ascension. The Indigenous have spoken about the coming changes to Earth and humans for generations.

Your job changes within the return of the light onto New Earth. I am here to remind you of who you are lest you forget. The light of the world that your beloved guides speak of contains the light of you as well.

All present in this moment upon New Earth are lighting up and receiving and lighting it up again. As the beacons you are, you pull in dark and light. You are the first receivers; humans and the trees receive the energy first when the light comes in. Simply ride the waves of strong plasma light flowing into the newly advanced human body. The year of 2022 was a magnificent testing ground to see how each one can work with the challenges that you all wrote and created for yourselves. What was known and experienced as accept/deflect or ignore happened when one took in a lesson and then sidestepped or rejected the lessons due to overthinking, judgment, or by putting hard times down to too much pressure from self, and/or others. Asking 'Why is this happening to me?' instead of 'What can I learn from this?' may slow down the lesson. Of course, as you know, you each wrote all of it to keep coming in like the tide until every bit of it is seen. You are now noticing the credits rolling by after 'the movie' of the last few years.

*Congratulations on sitting through that blockbuster! To remind you again and to answer that question, it's a big no! You do not know the ending of the movie. Isn't that glorious? ~ **Channeled from Archangel Metatron***

*Your mission is a relay race. Do your part and pass it on once you've completed what you came here to do. The light brings forth the shadows and the truth will out. There are choices this year, do listen to your heart and then choose, or not. Either way, you choose. ~ **Archangel Gabriel***

*You have made your move before. This is another time to move. If you trust, then go. Some people will always have the need to be taken care of. Contracts are held tightly and when they are removed, you will then see choices in more situations. Much will not be seen until it is time to be seen. ~ **St. Francis of Assisi***

*Love is your job. Remember, frequencies rise and fall. Follow these waves as a child would, staying in this moment without judgment. There is much to learn from the highest waves as well as the troughs. ~ **Seraphim Angel, Seraphiel***

I chose the path of the middle road years ago. In order to feel true freedom, I let go of relationships and situations that did not feel peaceful and cleared my life mentally and physically of clutter. I felt so much better afterward and much more like myself. I noticed people around me doing the same thing. Not all relationships are meant to last a lifetime.

The ascension into higher frequency is in full force now on planet Earth. Each human body and mind experience this evolution differently, as no one person is biologically exact to another. According to writers and visionaries, Diana Cooper et al (2010), we experienced The Cosmic Moment on Solstice, December 21, 2012. That day heralded an opening of accelerated human development. The ascension of planet Earth from 3D to 5D began in earnest.

Ascension symptoms vary as geomagnetic storms and solar flares occur much more regularly. Heading into solar maximum in 2024, an every 11-year-or-so cycle, we are now experiencing subtle organic changes, as well. We feel these changes happening now in our bodies almost daily.

As we pay attention to our bodies, we learn to take better care of ourselves and can then recognize when the body shows a pattern of needing more rest, water, and resources. Headaches, nausea, dizziness, sleeplessness, and more are common as symptoms during solar flares and geomagnetic storming.

*We greet you with respect for standing strong. Many are wobbling across the Earth with the onslaught of incoming plasma light. Whether this incoming light is perceived as positive or disarming, it comes anyway, does it not? So, it's up to you what to choose to believe about your light symptoms and the need to clear the physical vessel. Whatever you believe is causing your illness or stress right now it is best cleared with gratitude, love and belief in yourself. Appreciation and gratitude clear all. Stand in the solid belief that your heart knows the way to health. ~ **Nostradamus***

Your human body developed on its own as you matured. You did not have to concentrate to make it happen. The miracle of birth and death proves this point as well. Your beautiful human body is developing and changing in this new energy, day by day, on its own. Overthinking and focusing on how you are physically experiencing the ascension causes any discomfort to become more intense.

We shall explain why many humans feel the latest currents. Sensations run the gamut. One might feel a quick turning spin, a twist in the higher chakras and an influx of light, perhaps a bit of dizziness. If one resists the invitation of light, it is so much harder to process. Imagine having a cookie sheet on your head and standing in the shower expecting to get clean, then getting angry that the shower doesn't work today! When one accepts the light for the beautiful eventual result of clearing density and expansion, the shower feels like a beautiful cleansing release. Accept that as the increase continues, the human body can now hold a much higher frequency. It's so easy to label the experience something other than what it is; it is nothing but expansion. ~ **Nikola Tesla, Professor Albert Einstein, & Professor Stephen Hawking**

You may notice and feel 'the illusion'. It will be clunky, and to some it will be seen as a farce. You'll see it for what it is, the last gasp. The galaxy is full of change, the Earth as well. Of course it is! The pyramids, the water, and the land shall hold, but change will be everywhere. It is all very much alive and always has been; brilliant, green trees, bright, vibrant sky, and a feeling of celebration. The frequency may feel like a pulling and a vibration in your physical body. This can be true, both in an up frequency and down. The day's issues can feel chaotic so remind yourself to intend to be in the highest timeline in the now. What your body tells you is all the information you need in this moment. Humanity shall rise together, even beyond what has occurred. We know all of you are hurting. Hold your peaceful stance and do not be alarmed. The kingdom of heaven awaits. ~ **Chief Sealth, Duwamish and Suquamish, Washington State**

Walk forward with the sun. It is the original protection, the first light of strength. Release the mind's chatter so that the subtle whisper of your guides and higher self can come through easier. We are now in the Age of Aquarius! No more Cosmic Tough Guy Capricorn, telling us how things should go in the old ways! Some feel the ascension intensely, and some people not at all. But soon, no one will be able to deny the changes.

Trust the expansion of the light body to hold the frequency coming in. Remember, all is energy. Many will mistake the light for something else. This light influx has been prophesied for millennia. ~ **Nikola Tesla**

Of course, to understand solar events, you must remember there have been other big solar events upon earth. Each soul will experience the events differently, human and animal. Many of you have already experienced large solar events on your own. You have grown and have advanced your abilities. Recovery is needed afterwards, a time of rest. Survival is not the correct frequency; no fear is necessary. If the frequency seems difficult, tap your heart and remind your body you are taking care of it. Ask through your highest self that the energy is turned down. Pushing against the frequency causes the block. Rest, relax and allow. ~ **The Seraphim Hybrid Sara on Solar Events**

Warriors of Peace

My Team of Light reminds us to honor ourselves during the harder times. When times get tough, we must stay grounded in our heart and observe.

We send love and compassion toward all souls on Earth and beyond. Hold together in peace as the maelstrom surges around you. Remember who you are. You are not your abuser, your old enemy or your past, and yet, you will remember that there is only one human race when you see love in the heart of pain. Then you are free. Bring towards yourself peace beyond what is known. All that must be done is to trust. May God bless all today. ~ **Siddahartha Gautama, Buddah**

You are witnessing timelines meeting at a crossroads. As you go forward, more will be seen for what it is. There will seem to be plot twists. What did not feel positive to you and what is sticking in your craw is the deep underlying hatred within the movements. The anti-human points that you couldn't get past that were glossed over. The reason for these parts of the movements will become clear. Please do not fear. The light has seeped into all cracks and crevices and will illuminate it all. ~ **Reverend Dr. Martin Luther King, 8 January 2021**

Power is nigh for the humans now on Earth. You are seeing a great divide and if unity is to reign, each one must make the decision for peace. Peace over the Earth. Many are angry now or just scared. Those are limiting focused patterns that keep people stuck. You have seen how looping can stick you for hours or days. Remind all that old family dynamics, ancestral cords, programs and old contracts can be cleared right now in the blink of an eye. It is good to connect; we send our love to you today. We are grateful there are so many awakening to remember, but even the most powerful have had their heads turned by how great the pressure is at the moment. Step out, realign, and walk away if you need to. ~ **Nostradamus**

You are holding peace as a witness. All that is required now is your own grace as you see destruction of the old and new construction on New Earth. It is truly a revolutionary act to hold peace. The one who hears truth and recognizes it is as important as one who works for truth already. For soon they will be the same person. It is in timing to release one's experiences and allegiances, to all structures, family and friends if the relationships, contracts, and beliefs are over ~ **Archangel Gabriel**

Our guides teach us in timing. They move to the front and stay with us while we learn what is important to understand at that moment. Our spirit guides and ancestors are always nearby. They step forward, teach, and then step back again.

7 January 2023

In my vision, I am in a canyon. As my feet go round and round, I create a circle. My guide, Chief East Lee, tells me he is my only guide for now. I must sit with him over the next few days.

I listen to frequency music as he instructs me to focus in a different way. The bright blue sky is blocked by a huge rainbow ship of light. My neck and head are stretched back, as I rest on the scaffolding, he attaches me to. I feel a great pull. The Holy Ones are standing at the rim of the canyon. Instruction comes once by my throat toning guide, Juan. I am dancing, now free, and skipping around the canyon with my family. I view the body, stretched up and back at the bottom of the canyon. He tells me we will do this twice. The music transports me. The Chief says I am learning to hold great strength. I see the horses and the buffalo and the eagle.

Later that night, I couldn't sleep. My mind raced. The Chief told me to walk the grass circle again and bang the drum. I looked down. It's a copper pot and a wooden spoon. Ha! I did this until I relaxed and fell asleep.

The next morning I listened to the guides speaking about taking peaceful action.

The power resides within the people of the Earth. When any successful action triumphed, it was when humanity reached the tipping point of claiming a better way, and enacting that way forward. Your God-given right, your human ability, your own right to exist on a planet where the very air, water, food and products support you, begins with your voice. That voice must flow further than your living room. Action, I say, must be taken. Ideas in heads and action, not reaction in the hearts, inspire more than just writing and connecting through a video or on social media. This unique time on planet Earth serves two distinct purposes. Light and dark are seen clearly. What you do with this information is up to each one. Hold Earth and those who walk upon it in the highest peace. Observing with a clear view will change you. Allow this to happen by coming to your breath again and again. ~ **Benjamin Franklin, On What One Person Can Do**

Intend to see the lightness on Earth now. There are choices, very clear ones. Make the choice to foster peace. Yes, some need the illusion of safety. Let them have it. It is no one's path to say what is true for all people. ~ **Ascended Master Jesus Christ**

Attend now as a great connection has occurred. Star and Stone are close together. Follow through past Mother Gaia's crust into Inner Earth. See the trees that speak through the mycelium down into the blue glow. Now hold. The quiet you feel is not death, simply the absence of movement. Those who continue to hurry have missed this point. Not to worry or attend to them now. Soul, simply rest. ~ **Lord Ganesh, 2022**

The Shadow

Shadow work or looking within at your trauma is hard work and some of the best work you will ever do. To reach the upper dimensions is a great goal that I can only be attained by grounded, focused work on the darkness we have within the subconscious.

Some are not ready to look at their shadow. When one awakens, one is so excited and new and ready to look at the light! But a true awakening soul rigorously attends to their dark shadow self. The loud voices and up and down, energy shows this. Do not resist this important step. We are all at once light and darkness, ~ **Reverend Dr. Martin Luther King Jr**

What has been a focus falls away easily. Old rights and beliefs are seen for what they were: control and power over one another. Time adjusts and lengthens, even when the long path is before you. Walk the path with the intention to learn. Roadblocks can be turnstiles. Learning from what was the difficulty is now simply perceived as a place on the roadmap. The long walk contains both abundance and scarcity and all reflects growth. ~ **Ascended Master Jesus Christ**

When we hold peace in our hearts daily, it will be easier to rise up during turmoil. My guides often remind me that each challenge is just a temporary stopping point on the road. We don't need to camp there. Take a close look at your triggers. Receive them as a gift and a beginning place to dig in. Your shadow-self shows itself in layers. Keep going. Acceptance is a part of the process.

Stop Shooting Yourself in the Foot is a class I taught in April 2023 and is still available on my website. I sensed that time was speeding up to a gallop. And then boom! Roadblock.

This roadblock or a line you have not been able to cross was in timing for examination on the day of the class. We looked at why we stop ourselves right before advancement. This roadblock exists in the mental layer of the chakra system. Once cleared, the river runs easier. We spoke with goddess Ma-at about balance. She reminded us that our path has space for forward and backward motion. This is a journey with no need to label, judge or get stuck. It is simply the road of life.

Be easy on yourself! Allow others to have space to work out their own issues in the right timing for them.

*What is secreted in the sweet cake shall be different for each one as all have had a dark night. If one has worked diligently to hold one's energy and not to get wound up into the maelstrom, one passes easily up into the higher dimensions. Often one looks back afterward not knowing if an event has approached or has even happened. When people see what is actually true for them, there may be a lag time to sit with that truth. When the light turns up, sit with what is now illuminated until you can understand what has happened with all of your being. Pull the knowledge into your heart and find your own complicity. Graciousness, gratitude and a willingness to look at what frequency you hold allows the chaos to begin to clear. ~ **Holy Mother Mary, Universal Angel***

*There are groups congregating at this time for a reason. Why would people come together out of shared anger if there wasn't trauma suffered in the first place? Peace can be learned. Right now is a time where the world saw the result of hatred and many decided no, not me. Not anymore. When one chooses to heal, hatred and groups stuck together with the glue of shared trauma begin to unravel. This is what you're noticing. Keep noticing! There is the law of the land and also a spiritual law. You will be witnessing, retooling and relabeling. There will be but one law going forward. ~ **Saint Francis of Assisi, Summer 2020***

*We send love and compassion towards all souls on Earth and beyond. Hold together in peace as the maelstrom surges around you. It is truly the dawning of the new day. Bring towards you peace beyond what has been known. All that must be done is to trust. ~ **Siddahartha Gautama, Buddah***

*Warriors of light, you have the ability to withstand others' energies in a new way. Your heart is open in all the channels, and you await the next move up in ease. ~ **Nostradamus***

*We wish all beings health, happiness, and wholeness. There are so many souls awakening to remember! It is a glorious sight on Earth to see all the action! All of you deserve love and happiness and shall receive it. The moment the force field of fear drops, let it go, rip it up! In the peace that remains, remember who you are. When you see love in a heart of pain, you are free. May God bless you all today. ~ **Professor Albert Einstein***

A Different Kind of Service

You may sense that you are ready to make a change. Perhaps you are considering another type of work or a new way to be of service that doesn't cost more than you have to give.

Or perhaps staying in the same place with a new, open mind set will be what you choose.

Time is nothing. Do you understand that? Go forth as my representatives and know that I am with you at all times. Serve God as I do, begin to lay the foundation of the very path you will walk. Do it now and you shall have what you need. For some it is a voice. For some it is inner knowing. You shall have that and more. Brother versus brother, sister versus sister, neighbor and families fighting over old beliefs. See it in the layers and in the faces. You must walk forward past this, as all shall be known in timing. Your heart is upon humanity. Go forth, owing no man, owing no God, just divine love. This is my message today: go back to your daily way of being. We wish you to enjoy your body upon this Earth and know you have been anointed. You will build a future. Walk your path and walk it well. So, it is. ~ **Seraphim Angel, Seraphiel**

Shall we speak on judgment? For truly in the last few years there was much of it. It was a major force. At this moment the true test is how do you love yourself? Are you second, third or fourth in line in a dedication to caring for yourself? You must be first now for a reason that is the lesson of this year. The perception of others around you being your own cause of suffering is incorrect. You shall see this year that you have always held the key. So yes, judgment, self-love, non-acceptance of self, fighting, and resisting shall be part of what comes apart in the New Year. Of course, each has their own way of explaining this. And that may be an old way of dealing with it. The next phase has begun. What has been a focus falls away easily. Old rights and beliefs are seen for what they were; control, and power over one and another. Time adjusts and lengthens, even when the long path is before you. Walk it with attention to learn and gather and ease. With this intention, roadblocks can be turnstiles. Learning from what once was difficult is now simply perceived as a place on the roadmap. The long way contains both abundance and scarcity and all reflects growth. ~ **Ascended Master Jesus Christ, 2021**

It's a stubborn issue when you're stubborn. There's no other thing to do but to let go. ~ **Blue Star Beings Collective**

Life shows up to some as difficult and sometimes it's hard to remember that "this too shall pass". What one takes from current lessons will be instructive for life in this incarnation. As all are beginning to understand, their lessons after lessons are placed before the soul for growth. They are meant to be embraced, but at this time on earth, it just feels like a continuing rain down of problems, over and over, without ceasing. You asked, will we ever run out of issues? There will be a time on earth when humans will see why this time was so special, such a huge transition, and they will all look back on what they came through. You cannot see how the chains link up yet, though many try and then think they know. Do you trust? If you do, you will know deep in your heart that all is growth. Each 'new' problem has a key to it. Humans see patterns in other people in a clearer way than they can see their own. When you trust, you assist. Now is the time to understand that you must look further. Go back. ~ **Ascended Master Jesus Christ**

On this day, November 11, 2022, I released the frequency of war in my energy field and vessel. I released the grief, anger, regret, aggression of war from any lifetime when I have participated in the harming of any human or other in any lifetime or world. Though I laid my sword and shield down years ago, I remind myself that the tools of war are many and so I search myself for all aggression.

The lesson is compassion versus carrying too much weight on our shoulders that belongs to another person or time. I forgave myself for warring with words and losing myself in the fight with others, when backing away could have accomplished all I needed in peace and ease.

I hand the energy of war participation over to the light of God.

The middle road brings peace. Right or wrong is not the focus, the walk is the focus. ~ **Entirah Meh, Sirian Council of Light**

And when a line is drawn, one can walk forward. A simple yes or no brings peace. When one is on the fence, the energy is insecure. ~ **Archangel Michael Of The Sun**

Your Truth

You are directed to focus on the moment before the choice is made. That is a sweet spot, it is the timing and the goal. There will be signs. Decide right now that a decision will contain that pause and you'll make a better decision. This is where the human trips up; the human acts out of fear, stress, laziness or habit and then answers the question too quickly. The extra few moments taken before a decision is critical. You are worth that pause! You also have a moment to decide if you believe a story, don't you? Come into your heart. Ask yourself if it is true for you? You certainly know the frequency of gossip and catty conversations. Now flow that knowing towards the frequency of truth and energy accumulation. Stories go around, collecting up energy. ~ **Holy Mother Mary, Universal Angel Tells Us There Will Always Be a Choice**

My dearest, good morning! We are here with you. Do not despair. A mistake is all that was made. Your brain adjusts in these energies. Your body does as well. Feel the peace. We are the balance on earth. This awakening is upon us. My love, hold fast to your belief about this awakening. We have always been here! All can finally be seen. Not everyone shall agree, but where did we come from then if not here? It feels to you as if humanity went on vacation to the beach all at once. Do not tax the mind, you are just awakening further. ~ **Herve, Lyran Guide on Making Mistakes, Spring 2023**

The Tension of Growth Until Surrender

Lionsgate!

One of my favorite times on the yearly path opens on August 8. The lead up to it was always felt and we were able to view and clear what was being felt, that being judgment and the energy of the victim.

We are in the time of "getting out of our own way" – summer school! – in other words. During this time, we are ready to work with what comes up to be cleared at the moment we sense that there's something ready to see! Too long have we spent in the trenches of "I am not willing to see it!" Your life's photo becomes clear, and then sharpens. Soon there is no camera or television, no box – only the road directly in front of you! When you become your own Pinball Wizard, you dodge and weave and keep going, and then you notice life flows easier along your own road. There will always be challenges, but as a Wizard you just keep on going.

When we look at our shadow, we see where we have taken from others as well, where we have hung on for support and stayed there, rather than deciding to stand on our own. When we recognize our own power (versus the force), we come into balance.

Imagine an agility training course that a dog runs through. The dog is taken through a tight roll of cones, and up and over fences. Such concentration! But soon, muscle memory kicks in after doing the same thing for a few times. This also happens to humans! As we do our daily practices, it becomes something we do not want to miss because it feels so good. The body remembers how good it can feel with the practice done each day. You get used to meditation or walking first thing in the morning – the body craves that peace. But first, the decision is acted upon. If you approach in resistance to your practices, do something new or something you consider fun beforehand. You decide what is part of your Heaven on Earth. Soon you will not need to have confirmations or ask for clarity, or the need to know. The body will tell you all you need to know.

Remember, you are the human 2.0, at the very least! You are a brand-new unit now and if old stuff comes up again, remember, you have new and better tools. There's no need to panic or to loop back around. Just focus and clear what has come up. You represent your own divine self at all times. Professor Albert Einstein reminded me that he worked in a patent office applying legal principles. He said, "You are the judge, jury, executioner, defendant, prosecutor, and defense. You are the jailer as well as the dove."

July 2023 brought in the highest energy of the great Sun. We cruised, full throttle, no longer marooned on Fantasy Island. Illusions, inner and outer, dropping like it's hot during the Summer of Love. In my class called, "Pinball Wizard," I said we were in summer school with big cat mamas and daddies and the blue dogs from the Dog Star, Sirius. This was the time the world found a key to a door that unlocked the 777 portal on July 7, 2023. When a lock and key appear, a door shows up.

What did you do?

Vision:

I saw a long line of people. They wore pastel colors: blue, lavender, pink, gold, and diamond robes. They carried gifts. I saw Archangel Gabriel.

My dear, no time to waste! Lie down and visualize. ~ ***Archangel Gabriel and Holy Mother Mary, Universal Angels Explained to Me What I was About to Witness***

This visualization lasted hours. I saw a desert. So many people walked past me. I just observed. The Holy Ones told me that I witnessed a homecoming, a ceremony of thanks.

*Humanity reached the apex, a true merge of endings. More shall show up as the days progress. There will now be an opening, a time to see with empathy, fear and war for those that align with these frequencies. Dark versus light as it always has been. You are feeling each other's fears. People of Earth are not the same this year nor as they were in any other year. Time has moved on, and war is no longer acceptable. Bullies, sanctions, mandates, forced closures, FORCE of any kind; it's all over when you say "No!" Now is the time for peace and helping one another. The frequency of war has been popping up; yes because it's global reach is known and relied on for control since time began. All shall fall, all is in timing. The author of war is the one in the background; he is the idea of pain and force. They see themselves at the helm when in reality they are leading from out-of-power, invisible and safe. The apex is the common man or pawn. Today the pawn resists. The pawn takes the Queen now. ~ **Nostradamus further explanation***

*Dear Ones—A reset has occurred, and timing requires rest as all gather together again. This is the time of inner reflection and release of old beliefs and mucked up energy, inside and out. The mind follows. If this process happens in ease, then the next step will show itself. All shall be revealed in the brightest light ~ **Lord Kumika, Chohan of the Blue Ray***

The Blue Light

*The blue light arrives, just as the prophecies have foretold. The world felt the arrival. Illusions clear from the inside and the outside. ~ **Nikola Tesla***

If you are interested in the blue light's arrival on planet Earth, visit the work of Nancy Rebecca on Blue Light Movement on Facebook and YouTube (2023). Nancy's website is listed on the Metaphysicians and Groups page.

*The pink light of the Stargate supports all in love. True creativity can flow in its resonance. The heart and mind entrain in its frequency. The Stargate pushes all by way of a peaceful motion. The pink light supported the incoming blue light. Within this work, the Violet Flame is the motivator of clearing in the zero point field. Your body is your teacher. ~ **Holy Mother Mary, Universal Angel***

Winter Solstice, 2022

Today is open for self-care, rest, cleansing and happy pursuits. For in the next few days all shall feel a lightening of spirit in all around you. Constant worry stops. Truly, the blue light is upon Earth.

*This day brings in the transformation of the child within. This is an expanse allowed by the galactic codes flooding into humanity. The truth of the divine feminine and the divine masculine combines in real time now within us, and the third energy of self comes forth. This is the birth of creativity and realignment with Source of All. The golden path is renewed. Go now to your temple of creation and see the new abilities, colors, visitors, and energy available to you. Add to creation your highest desires of service. The Codex that you saw today is a new code. This is the Akashic records, third eye and healing code. ~ **Ascended Master Jesus Christ***

The Council of Nine

The council of nine is a group of my guides that have been with me my entire life and in many lifetimes. In this year of 2023, they speak in a group:

*As you understand that more can be done in a group, you understand as above and so below. This time before us shall be historic as timelines close and souls shall go further into what is yet unknown to humanity. The human body is feeling in ways it has never felt before. Brother pitted against brother for the right to breathe freely. Humans are in fear for their lives and their death, but all is in perfect timing as each goes through the stages the collective needs to go through to grow. Do not fret, as you shall continue to feel pulled, but instead look back at just how far you've come. If the sensations are painful, request a lessening or support for the vessel in a calmer way. Stay still right now and allow the passage of this amazing energy to flow through you. Do not fear! My appearance has changed as well! I am a representative of the Divine Feminine. All are welcomed into the glorious clear light of the new day. Earth is returning to balance now. Many times, the attempt has been made to align all within the light. Now, the final tipping point is here. You shall all be able to make miracles now. This is a human divine right. Your view of who you are is multi-dimensional now. You are in the driver's seat. ~ **The Morrigan**

What Goes Up

Remember, after every timeline shift, every personal healing, and energetic jump into higher energy, there may be a time of realignment. This may feel like a temporary fall. Don't worry—energy supports, and you will easily rise again.

What Happens After a Timeline Shift?

You will notice changes in color and new sensations during your first meditation of the day. If there was a timeline shift, you will feel physically and mentally better, lighter. You may notice the things that you have had on your plate the day before are simply unimportant or now easier to handle. Answers to questions will come easier.

When we reach a personal or collective timeline shift, there may be a correction in our human bodies before leveling up again. It is important to remember that continued practices are imperative at these times.

As we grow, it is easier to ride the wave of the increased solar and Earth energy. As the body develops and changes, this will become even easier. The day continues with prayer, meditation, and energy work just like any other day. Time is needed to rest the body, hydrate, and recover.

Second Shift Sleep

In the last few years, sleep has changed for many of us. There are nights that sleep doesn't come at all. I find that welcoming these nights, and the curious feeling the next day as if I've actually traveled and still feel fine, is something to celebrate.

This is the key to thriving without a traditional sleep pattern. Complaining lowers our energy—then more examples to complain about will show up in front of us! Words call in what appears around us. Just think of your cell phone when you talk about buying anything these days. Pretty soon several examples of the coveted object "just happen" to show up! So, complaining about sleep or these new transitions does not help us work through the transition or become more attuned to how things will feel and show up in the next transition.

Going to bed early and waking up to write or read in the early hours, and then return back to bed again, seemed to be the norm for much of 2023 and beyond.

Nothing is fixed in place until or unless we say it is! And then, it still might not be. The urgency to find an answer is displaced by our seeking an answer. Rest and relax through these changing times. It is the only way.

Many fell for someone or something placing thoughts and beliefs in their way, until embraced as their own. Acknowledge this when it happens, forgive yourself, and move on.

Then there were the things we all fell for and enthusiastically embraced as general truths. That list is big, and all must find out for themselves what is really true in one's own timing.

The time is now to embrace changes in health and move into peace and ease. There is divine support for us to do so. Listen to the voices of my Teams of Light as they speak here and always listen to your own inner voice and teams. Believe that you have all that you need inside your heart. Always use discernment to determine what is true, as some may not be true for you.

Learning to hold your frequency

For many lifetimes, we, as healers, hold or pass people's pain and illnesses through our own body to clear. This is an old way and should no longer be used. Years ago, the guides asked me if I was ready to stop this. I did not know I had continued the practice. You might notice this as your client clears something and now YOU have pain, discomfort, or tossed up emotions. It is time to stand in your own power with a peaceful edict and a solid path. The road is open for a new way. No one holds you back but you. The golden armor is yours to wear. If this old way of healing feels like what you are experiencing, accept that you are holding others' energy and make the decision to tap into universal energy instead of electing to use your own.

Whether you believe in armoring yourself or believing in clearing the energy you take in immediately (or both), remember that the human energy field is porous. We are portals. We must remember to clear ourselves each and every time we notice energy infiltration.

People need you and you need them, but you have now changed from an enabler to a lover of souls. Now you can truly assist people. Many had to learn that they must not enable others or do the work for them. Each person's lessons are to be learned by themselves. ~ **Ascended Master Jesus Christ**

Love flows constantly towards you. Revel in it. Do not look back! You know the past is a trap. The only way is forward. All hearts know this but forget in the illusion that it is actually a habit to look to the past. Break the habit of looking at the past. Those who did not continue the journey with you have their own journey. Remember this as you still hold onto the past. Take it as your job today to release all who hurt you in the stream of peace available today. May God be close to you as you do it. ~ **Nikola Tesla**

Our dear ones, the morning sunlight plays over Earth, lighting up the new growth. Visions of Spring with the possibilities of new growth on the trees and the land. Know your own tender, new shoots of confident growth and feel the wonder of change both over the Earth and within you. There is no stopping it. Yes, hard rain comes with the gray clouds that descend into the valleys, but does that moment stop the tree from its seasonal shifting? Nor should it stop you. Part of your growth is within the stages of comfort and discomfort, for in the hardship, the possibilities of change push in and the release is sweet. Step aside for Nature's turn is upon you for quiet inspiration and marvel on this new day. There is a cave I know. Once per day for a short while, it was lit entirely by strong light. At other times the dark flooded in. The light within my soul sustained me. It is now your choice to hear a message and hear it clearly from the heart. If it is your message, and the voice is loud and clear, take the wind where you will. Call in Jesus. Work together, for there is more to learn. Children of peace, drop your sword. No more are you chased. The mind releases if you let it. All assistance is here for you through your own Family of Light as we are here and will always be. ~ **Mary Magdalene**

Dear one, the Shekinah Glory is upon you. Now it is up to you. Still the mind and hold others in true peace for the kingdom is here. ~ **Ascended Master Jesus Christ, Explaining a New Way of Healing. It Took Me Month to Develop, but Now it Can be Instantly Accessed**

The possibility of still thought shall be so much easier for all here within the zero point field known to us as the light. As you all have experienced, the frequencies needed for healing are in the light and sound. However, the zero point stillness holds both, but the sound may not be available to each, as yet. Listen to no thoughts, feel into the color of pearl and diamond plasma and the essence of no time. Does this sound right to you? Judge not; think no thoughts, practice over and over and the peace will come forward. ~ **Holy Mother Mary, Universal Angel**

Remember, walk the middle path in peace with your eyes on the horizon. The shift into the ascension has happened. You are here and part of it. There is no doubt you are here for a reason. Let that reason be peaceful support of the planet, yourself and those around you.

CHAPTER 3

Your DNA and the Abundance Codes

Our DNA can be programmed by words and energetic healing, visualizations and sound. We are meant to return to a natural state of good health. We can create our own healing language of love and abundance and use it daily to remind our bodies and energetic fields to thrive.

Speak from within your heart and speak up with the unified language of energy and love.
~ President Mandela

"In my highest self, holding the highest frequency, I recognize that I'm truly ready to be real and authentic, the divinely fully embodied whole that I am.

I welcome my daily spiritual practice.

I release the trauma that has caused me to search outside myself, live for another and engage in behaviors averse to my soul's truth and highest human potential in this lifetime.

I am whole and unbroken. My soul is perfectly made.

I am ready to release what is not mine in a way I could not before. I am willing to see all of myself clearly and live in peace. It is my practice that holds the key.

In this lifetime, I choose myself." ~ Channeling for a friend

The Body Speaks

We have learned that we can speak to all parts of our body and make changes happen. We can speak, pray, and sing to help the body to relax. It is especially important to remind the body that it is safe and that we are paying attention to it. Acceptance of all of our body processes is important. The body then recognizes that we are acknowledging what is going on rather than pushing it away or fighting against it.

We can teach our body to accept what is about to happen by lovingly explaining that we are about to make a change or sit within a meditation for health. It is always important to visualize your body as whole and healed.

We can reprogram all parts of the body for growth and better health. Our bodies speak up with pain, illness, and exhaustion. We must learn to listen. If the mind is busy, sometimes a whisper isn't heard. Getting to know your body is imperative.

A pendulum is a great tool to dowse your levels and needs:

- How tired am I right now?

- Do I have enough water or food on board?

- Do I need a short rest, meditation or nap?

- Does this food and drink align with frequency and my body

Your DNA

Within the AOYE work, we have a skill called, "The Ladder." The skill is presented along with the other new skills in chapter 13.

DNA is also shown to me clairvoyantly as a ladder. In the class called, "Taking Steps Toward Love," the ladder symbol shows up before us made of crystal and bright gold that shines with the light of rainbows. As we climb the first ladder in the journey, we then traverse over to the next by a bridge and then on to the next ladder and beyond. It is easy to see the connecting bridges. Then codes are released.

As humans evolve, the number of DNA strands increase.

Meditation

In the past, you've done the work to heal yourself, unacknowledged, during sleep and the few moments you have allowed for yourself here and there in meditation. In the past, we could sit in meditation once in a while and do some grounding when we thought about it. We could get away with eating lower-energy foods and supplementing here and there. But in the last few years, we have come to know this as an old way. While useful for growth in the past, it will no longer be enough.

If you are a regular meditator, you will notice after a time of daily focused meditation, you will begin to go in a direction towards opening up with new colors and visions. You'll be able to see the next step to take for releasing and returning back to yourself. You will become used to taking that time for yourself, as it is the best part of the day now, and you'll crave the relaxation and revitalization of meditation.

Even 30 minutes of meditation per day can assist with returning and building energy. Check this out for yourself. In the afternoon or in the early evening when you become tired and notice how you feel, sit in meditation and then afterwards, dowse your level of sleepiness or exhaustion. You might be surprised! You might think you need a couple of hours to nap, but really, 30 minutes of meditation is enough to make a big difference.

If you are just starting to meditate, try different types of meditation online or in a group. You may like to focus on music, chanting, or maybe a voice that leads you on a guided meditation. I still do these types and like to mix it up. Every day I rest in meditation, and it helps me to be relaxed and I find I get more done. I am happier if I make time for my meditation practice.

Beliefs and Programs

You are running up against a belief. ~ **Nostradamus**

Ask yourself: Do you believe you can heal your own body? This is the $64,000 question, isn't it? Are you a healer with a stubborn, recurring issue or condition that you just haven't been able to heal 100% or maybe you can get the issue to go away for a little while and then it comes back? Maybe you help others successfully, but you can't seem to clear up your own illness.

As healers, we believe that we can help people that are suffering if they ask us to do so. This is the key in my opinion. I believe someone who asks me to work with them must make the time to be available (and then be willing) to take in the healing energy and, sometimes, homework.

This is why I do not send remote energy healing without people's permission. We all have free will. It is tempting to send energetic healing to someone, but the individual has free will. They may not be in the right time to receive energy healing or even be open to it. This may also have little to do with belief. I find that energetic healing can help people whether they believe in this type of healing or not. Can we help everyone? No! The most important thing to remember is that we must not have judgment around whether a person heals or does not heal.

The human body's natural state is health. As we use the AOYE system, the codes will bring out beliefs, programs, past life issues and more.

A person may hold a belief that they cannot heal, and they may not know it. Perhaps this is from a past life. One example of a program might be a person who has the same illness as their mother or grandmother. Yes, this can be genetics, but it can also be a belief that they will end up as their family member with a certain type of illness or disability.

If you use the codes every day, and for several days you receive the same symbol, know that you are going deeper. When the symbol changes, you have released whatever blockage you had. For example, as I work on myself each day, I may find that code #41 (Power Back) repeats. This means that I am going deeper to return my power from where I lost it somewhere along the path. During the day I could think about the time of lost power, but easier still would be to declare at night that I am willing to dream about that time and release it. The body works with the given code for three days and the code may or may not repeat. Remember to support your body with water and rest as it works to release with the gentle power of the AOYE codes or overlays.

What Happens When You're Out of Your Body?

Have you ever felt lightheaded right after a shock or an accident or even an argument? A stressful situation may cause part of the soul to release out of the body temporarily. This may feel like the sensation of coolness and a "rising" feeling, almost like losing consciousness. Simply call yourself back: in body, mind, spirit, and emotions while tapping your heart. This will reset your soul after dream travel or a shock. I do this upon awakening in the morning or during any stressful incident.

When I look at clients under great stress, sometimes I can see an outline of a silhouette of their body near their own physical self that tells me they are out of their body. The next step is grounding. Then we work on polarity.

An easy way to return polarity is to grab a metal spoon and run a figure 8 design on the bottom of your feet. I also begin every meditation by visualizing that I am standing on a figure 8 or infinity symbol inside the selenite bowl, my symbol for zero point. This is a visualization built into the opening of every reading, healing or meditation. Then make the statement out loud, "I call back polarity." You can immediately feel the difference.

The Abundance Overlay

There are six abundance codes. They are used by themselves for specific ways to increase abundance. They are used in groups, and they also show up in the Abundance Overlay. The Abundance Overlay was the very first overlay I saw in late 2023. I saw it form right in front of me. When added to another person's energetic field, they can feel tingling coming in from their feet to their head. It was explained to me that the overlays contain feminine energy to balance the codes which are masculine.

Of course, overlays and codes can be used separately but there is even more power and balance when used together.

*The overlays balance the body systems allowing the energy of the codes to be accepted easily into the human totality. The energetic platforms that show up in the overlays and the Grounding and Reunification that begins all Art of Your Energy work are 6th and up to 12th dimensional in form and are used to journey and hold space for healing. ~ **Nikola Tesla***

I teach classes in meditation and journeying which are available
on my website: www.maribeckman.com.

We met Goddess Ma-at at the River of Life in my class called "The Things We Do/Don't Do for Love" in February 2024. The Goddess directed us to notice a scale in front of us in the river. On the right side of the scale there was a pan where we were to put a symbol from past relationships and situations that have a hold over us. She directed us to open our throat and tone or hum until a symbol formed in our hands. She asked us to lay down the sacred representation of all the pain upon the golden pan on the right side of the scale.

She asked us to be brave.

Then we toned for 30 seconds to manifest our own symbol of creation. As we toned, hummed or spoke in the language of our own soul, we noticed the symbol that formed in our hands. This was our own creation of energy in form.

It was time to take the symbol and place it on the golden pan on the left. She directed us to look to our right and, behold, we noticed the vessel of pain symbol disappeared!

What took its place was the alchemized pain turned into creation that formed a symbol of abundance and rested on the pan to the right.

I was astounded at the simplicity and perfection in this direct alchemization of pain into abundance. Releasing fear showed me the door. Creativity is the key.

Dearest ones, mighty ones. Trust the elders, the ancestors and this body you are in in this lifetime. You were sent forward to heal and you are able to do so. You are still thinking too shallowly. Rise up into the power, you are embodied now and ready to speak up. Your voice will quiver, speak up anyway. You are backed by your elders and your family from generations ago. Look for their strength in yourself. The fragile families you came from were a mirror shattered by you, years ago. It was time for both sides of that mirror to grow or not to grow. Your prison of thought is no more. Are you ready?

Do not be afraid. Fear is a lie that the mind invests in to keep you comfortable in your own stagnation. Those who look to blame or judge so shall see this as no forward movement. Patch up your broken heart now. Send forth the healing to your soul group and future self. Redouble your effort. See yourself recovered, free and abundant. You get to that day with inner work, and everyone must do it. If you keep on seeing your pain as separate from yourself, you will continue that pain, or you can choose right now to change your focus and love it back into true health. You have enough to thrive.
~ **Goddess Kali**

There is a step on the path where you will not think of physical pain, chronic illness, or anything that has been part of your body aside from health. One day you will notice that you are feeling better. Many years ago, a friend told me that my foot pain was like a big pile of dirt in my yard. He advised me to make a plan each day during energetic healing to take a shovel of dirt and remove it from the pile. Soon, I will see the pile is no longer there. Keeping your mind on health and having a little fun goes a long way to change the energy of an illness.

CHAPTER 4

Health and Healing Your Four Body System

Many of us who are here on Earth at this time have experienced health issues. We may have fallen on our knees as it hasn't been a cake walk to be one of the points of entry for the incoming light. We are learning how to help ourselves back up onto our feet as our strength grows daily now.

This time of ascension has not been easy on the physical body. ~ **Chief Sealth, Duwamish and Suquamish, Washington**

Nikola Tesla: Behold your box of pain. Are you ready?
Me: But I can't build myself back with that!
Nikola Tesla: Precisely!

Not stubborn, exactly; willful. Willful shows up as stubborn if you go against the grain. Remember this is part of the lesson in this lifetime. Stand up for yourself peacefully. ~ **Master Li Shizhen (Dongbi), Master of Acupuncture.**

The Body

A Note I Wrote to Myself:

I love you, body of mine! Yes, others have loved you well, or not. But I treasure you. You and I are ascending together. We are each other's buddy in this lifetime.

I love you, scars and marks and sags!

I love the roadmap of life drawn on your skin.

I love you, feet, in your imperfection. But are you really imperfect? I love how we walk forward together and even when we take a step backwards, I love you then, too. It's a human thing.

I love how you react to kindness. I love the bloom of your heart in the presence of kindness and the dead truth. I love how you weed out the BS. I love you, my brain. So many told you that you didn't work right, that you were damaged from trauma, but those times were the lessons! I love that you just keep on learning and discovering! I love how you can think differently and spit out some cool stuff once in a while. I honor you when you are done for the day.

I honor you, stomach, and my earthen brain. You just couldn't stomach treatment from certain directions and broke under the weight of it. But by listening to your/my emotions and by my holding you well; you were able to heal.

I love you, wonky leg. You are a great teacher!

I honor my body today. I remember when it didn't receive any consideration and those were learning times, too.

I honor you, fluffy body. You are learning how to heal and let go in the presence of those who treasure you.

It's safe to release extra pounds that you held onto as protection. I will no longer tear you down for making choices of food to change your brain chemistry to fight pain. That was an old illusion, and we don't need to do it anymore. Now that the brain and body are being nourished and my attention is being paid to you, you can just relax. No more judgment about your appearance.

Once I accepted that the key is within me, my body relaxed and is letting go. I honor its ongoing transformation.

*As the light flows onto Earth, you all shall feel ups and downs in your body and systems. Flow with it! It is the only way forward! Like a boat on choppy seas, no resistance is required. A loose-limbed body, easy posture and a pure heart allow for freedom in the day. ~ **Ascended Master Jesus Christ***

*My dearest ones, you have traveled a long road to arrive at this point. Weary, but excited at the prospect of real change, the warrior doesn't pause at the crossroads, but charges on. Instead, warriors of light, may I instill in you a reflex to pause, slow down and make a concerted effort to bring yourself back to center early each day before the day's challenges begin? Take stock on what resources you hold, your level of light that you carry daily and your own nervous system's balance. You wouldn't drive your car without oil in it, would you? It's detrimental to the body to keep pushing along without a real rest and a top up of vital fluids and light. Earth, precious and new, is your battery. Bring your feet to earth. Bring your body to water in every way you can think of; for this is your element of peace. The very air outside is your breath. Quell the fire of the day each day and remember that a soldier of light is, at one's deepest essence, a team player in today's game. Lean on your support. Call Us to you. You are not alone. Take our sword, if you must fight for freedom, as you are better armored than you think you are. ~ **Saint Joan of Arc***

I love my first meditation in the early morning! It sets up the day, and it shows me how I have changed overnight. The morning view is my truest truth. You cannot miss the peace in a glorious new morning of possibilities! Just look around you! The colors are vibrant, the sun is brighter. If you cannot see this happening out of your window, then look inside of you.

*Rest and relax. The frequency is vast, but you now can support it. Even months ago, the human vessel would have reacted in a harsher way but great progress has been made. Do not allow your head to be turned by naysayers. Reach out as your family of true light is there to hold you. This is not humanity's time to go small. This time right now is the time seers have spoken about for generations. You are on the front row to this awakening. We acknowledge your anxiety and physical pain. We recommend that you not load your plate with tasks right now. Rest and reach out for support. The frequency is high, and you can choose to find peace in it. ~ **Seraphiel, Seraphim Angel**

Learning to understand what is going on around us through the ways in which the body reacts has been a step we all have to make. There were many seers that prophesied certain steps to watch out for as we began the ascension path years ago. We cultivated discernment with the understanding that the future is viewed through focus, beliefs, and the past trauma that each person carries.

2021 showed us that a stronger message to consider is how one feels inside the body. It has been ever-changing from ascension flu to incredible vibration and toning in the ears to higher skills coming online

Some of us needed that long walk of stubbornness to finally accept a clean diet and exercise program. That still voice inside me, and the louder voices of my guides, explained to me that small changes add up.

I also heard clearly that if I did not release certain things from my diet, my body would begin to act up, and act out loudly.

Then there is the matter of needs not being met with the daily diet that I was currently eating. A simple hair analysis a few years ago was eye-opening.

Regular cleansing and intermittent fasting can be valuable. For example, the four-body system; body, mind, spirit, and emotions can be separately dowsed with a pendulum each day to see which system needs the most attention.

A balance each day of a clean and healthy diet, enough water, exercise, meditation, and creativity can return one to a state of better health.

Mind

Our minds hold us captive. Change your mind and change your life!

*One must drop the cloak of separateness. You are all a part of this global family. Act as such. Stop fighting yourselves and fewer fights will show up around you. ~ **Holy Mother Mary, Universal Angel***

*It is important to hold what you are considering in the golden light of all love, freedom and possibility. In this light, all things that are viewed in hindsight will have come to pass in ease. If one focuses on restrictions, the energy of 'stop and worry' comes up. None of that is needed. Just do your best to focus on possibilities and mirror out what it is you want to see. ~ **Ascended Master Jesus Christ on Restrictive Thinking or Restrictions***

We humans have realized that limited thinking stops growth, and we are beginning to recover what wasn't available to us in the past years.

Beliefs and programs

Some beliefs we hold close are not even our own! Challenge yourself and see if this is true!

When one worries about when, where, or how the mind goes to turmoil. This action just does not align with peace. ~ **Nikola Tesla**

Be ready for strong mirrors of self. Things that make you uncomfortable, angry, fearful and shaken can be truly happening or, as you know, placed into a group consciousness to continue anger and fear, etc. Be willing to see those examples and sit with them. Take your lessons from the frequency and if you are ready, move on. There's no need to be pulled into dissatisfaction along with the collective stir up. This shall continue until it is seen for what it is; it is all just energy. Hold your own frequency in stillness. That which is stirred up has been so successful in the past to keep people off balance. The middle path does not require blinders so choose peace for yourself over and over. ~ **Ascended Master Jesus Christ**

Are you next? Am I? The door is in front of you. Do you take it? Then take it; see what is the next step. When the world around you shakes in fear or congratulates itself on what fails, look at yourself first. Did you have a part in it? If not, move on. This situation is not yours, and it never was. But if you did take part in whatever is causing that feeling in your body, or you witness a confrontation, it is up to you to then decide 'Is this mine?' Then go to work if it is. If it is not yours, step aside; all have enough going on that is actually theirs to adjust. Keep walking forward for a path may hold loops and backward steps. Every step is as important no matter, backwards or forwards and can hold truth. ~ **Mahatma Gandhi on Being Torn Down, Maligned or Canceled**

The Spirit and The Soul

Your spirit communicates with you and that small voice, once heard, will always be easily accessed with quiet focus.

The spirit is not the soul. Your soul is ancient and eternal and lies within as well as outside the body. It adjusts and readjusts, along with all parts of you, including your constantly changing chakras. The soul is many times your Earthly size, and only some of your soul exists within the human body. Rest assured, your soul is perfect and believes that you are perfect, too!

As the process of embodiment unfolds, more of one's soul is seated within. This is accomplished with clearing and returning practices, a beautiful and ongoing walk.

Your soul shines like burnished gold. It exists only in love, the love of you. The soul is a student of God. Your soul's existence should never be doubted. ~ **Archangel Michael of The Sun**

Dearest, feel. The soul is. God is. ~ **Holy Mother Mary, Universal Angel**

Emotions

Bear Medicine, from a Reading of a Friend:
Dearest warrior of peace, speaking up changes everything! You will no longer be silent and full of emotion, rigid and stuck. You will be flowing easily. Roar! Barge in. Be as a child who has needs because all people do, and yours are valid. Be unchained and unapologetic. Sound is life! Nature is rarely silent. Sing like the frogs…it's springtime!

Make sure that your emotional needs are being met by allowing yourself to feel those beautiful emotions! That's why you are here on Earth—the ability to feel. Take note, whether you are numbing out with any type of substance rather than taking a good close look at how you really feel. Remember, a substance can be alcohol, recreational drugs, food, sex, shopping, or a situation like staying overly busy in order to *not* have time to feel. Only you can determine what is causing pain.

Make sure to ground every day. Check whether the emotions you are feeling are actually yours. If you are around a person who is regularly angry, in deep grief for long periods of time, anxious, or depressed, there is always a chance you might be holding their emotion in your energy field. This is one of the biggest reasons why we stop and clear ourselves every day, multiple times daily. Ground several times per day, at a minimum. By bringing in the columns of light and working with color and frequency, you can make this a fun habit to get into.

You owe it to yourself to work diligently to create and preserve a happy life. You may need to make some big changes, but the moment you put yourself first or at least near the top, your life can't help but change for the better.

*Optical illusions abound. What is the truth? Truth can only be recognizable through the heart. The love frequency is the ground floor. There is much more. Breathe through fear and eventually one reaches bliss. ~ **Ra***

Of course, bliss and euphoria are passing emotions. Celebrate when you recognize that you are simply happy!

What is a boundary to some may look like a cage to you. It is valid to both. Battle lines could still be drawn, but it is a lower frequency. The path continues. Accept that you may need to release people and situations.

Though lessons still pour in, the lesson here is finished now that you realize you are done with certain individuals and situations. Your karma has concluded between you. The contracts are now void. Only love remains, and what you shall do now that the battle lines have disappeared, and the frequency has shown itself is to be love, this is your decision. Will you observe and return love?
*~ **Goddess Kuan Yin, Bodhisattva of Compassion***

It is now time to learn that all people in your life are the captains of their own destiny and they hold the blueprint of their soul, their own story. Another outsider can help only just so far. We are not here to learn other people's lessons.

Trauma, Timing, and Finding the Root Cause

Your momentum increases as you learn how to move on from the past. This being said, all lessons are fruit for understanding why we feel the way we do.

Your emotions are just as valid and as varied as anyone else's emotions. You may have been driven to hold back—to "appear clear and solid." Of course, there were points in life when you were driven to speak up. But when you didn't speak up, your mind and body felt the brunt of your holding back.

Self-love has moved into self-respect now. If this is the moment you have thought to put yourself first, it could be a bit unsettling. You may go back into your heart to see if love is still there. Give yourself all the time it takes.

*The feelings you have are valid. People have hurt you. You are also here because of what happened in your past, and you know it. Somewhere between the pain and the higher view is peace. Accepting yourself as who you are; is the key. What do you love about yourself? How can you embrace all of yourself without the pressure of family or friends' expectations of you? Nothing else could have been done. A complete split was correct for you. Look at your growth right now, you are healed, body and heart. A previous resistance to clearing the body stems from the need to control. You were trying not to feel the deep pain of abandonment. You were taken for granted that you were crazy, worthless, a drain, unreliable. This is hard to see because you are not these things. You were judged harshly. Are you ready to clear it? ~ **Ascended Master Jesus Christ**

Remember to call out to your celestial family for your needs. You will be able to see clearly when you are ready. Feeling safe will allow this to happen.

*Love is given as an offering from the Celestial Realm. We will meet you when your heart is open and even when walled off from pain and trauma. We will be there when you are in fear and experiencing loss. Yes, the time is now to open your eyes as all will be easier seen. Do not look away from the grief of others, for your heart may be strengthened in the love of those around you, who hold the frequency of peace. Fear weakens the human. It is an attractor, a lighthouse for more fear and the possibility of the body to read the truth in a skewed way. ~ **Holy Mother Mary, Universal Angel**

Trigger Happy

Celebrate the times you get triggered! Those moments are ripe and full of information.

There will be stuck emotions, often layered. Dig 'em out! We must always look at ourselves when triggered.

*Power is high for the human being upon Earth. Many are seeing a great divide. If this divide is to close and unity is to reign, each one must make the decision for peace, not just peace within but peace over the Earth. Many are so angry now or just scared. This is a limiting, focused pattern that keeps people stuck. You've seen how looping can stick a person for hours, days or longer. When pressure is high and heads are being turned by how great the pressure is, step out, realign and walk away. If one doesn't wish to be in a war, one must step back and allow the war to go on without them. ~ **Nostradamus**

Jealousy is a reaction out of deep trauma over lifetimes. An old lifetime, rubbing up against yours, making sparks. ~ **Chief Sealth, Duwamish and Suquamish, Washington State on Jealousy:**

The ego and personality are where the hinge resides. Where ego lies, roadblocks are visible. One must believe there is a world beyond what we cannot see. This is the true release of a holding pattern.

When the ego is still in force, there will be a reaction when one is up against a dilemma. Reactions of anger and threats may come. For the person to transform there must be a willingness to do so.

Becoming A Powerful Creator Being

In 2020, more of the world became empathic. This may have been scary for some people. It might've been a trigger-athon for folks who could not hold their energy solidly. As the heart opens, it may feel like pressure in your throat or in your chest. There were many, many of us that had fear in 2020.

Remember, triggers are your friends. They are what alert you to the next thing to clear up. Look at each beautiful emotion! And then remember, when was the first time you felt the emotion or who labeled you early on. Maybe you were labeled too logical, having no emotions, over emotional, or too sensitive! Someone else may have said this, and it is not true. Or maybe you really *are* sensitive! Remember, empathy is a superpower.

Safely releasing emotions with a trusted human is a divine act. We all need each other right now.

Your ego may be avoiding responsibility. If you take on someone else's emotion, that emotion now belongs to you. There is no more projecting onto someone else or blaming them for an emotion that you willingly took from them. "You have to feel it to heal it," as the old saying goes. The pendulum will teach you everything you need to know about emotion.

Does your workspace feel clean and clear? Do you feel energetically supported in the room in which you are working? Remember to clear your workspace and home every day.

Labeling

Stop complaining! Energy 101 tells us that what we focus on grows. Same for worry! Worrying is like riding a stationary bike from your house to mine. It's not going to get you anywhere.

People love to label each other! Maybe, in your family growing up, you were labeled the *smart one*, the *pretty one*, the *athletic one*, or the *peacemaker*.

Look around for labels on yourself. Begin to recognize where you label others and situations. It's a sticky thing to do. Labeling stops energetic flow.

Today is a day of peace in the in-between. Take this day and feel into it. Your burdens will be there tomorrow if you wish to pick them back up. But what if you called burdens 'expectations' then realized it was a label, and then you could simply have the opportunity to change things? Why wouldn't you? What could you change? Your mind, for one thing. Practice releasing some old, outdated belief that *you learned as a child or that society taught you. You will then come up to a higher view of what you are working with; that you call a burden. Today you have this challenge. Take the peace of the day and relax into the thought that you have created all of this. Easy and hard, bitter and sweet, positive or negative, are all lessons in labeling. ~ **Archangel Michael of The Sun***

Communication

Are you a good communicator? Can you do it under stress, tension and confrontation?

*Clear communication is often overlooked at the moment when emotions are high and pain is in the forefront. If you need to know something, ask and do not guess. Double thinking is trying to figure out what another person thinks or means. It is so much simpler, and way more time effective, to just speak up. ~ **Nikola Tesla***

Fear and Anger

Which one did you bring in with you as your "go to," number one emotion? This emotion will be the one that shows up when you are challenged or triggered.

Fear

*Does one need to see a disaster or Armageddon to believe? If so, one will have it. Do you walk forward in peace in the high frequency that is already available? If so, then no fear is needed. It is a personal daily decision. ~ **Chief Sealth, Duwamish and Suquamish, Washington State***

*The emotion of fear is appropriate in some situations just like every other beautiful emotion. When fear is held in the human body for even a short period past "Hey! Pay attention! Take steps and be aware!" then this emotion can become locked in. Humanity is ready to clean that up. ~ **Nikola Tesla***

*There is nothing more polarizing than the fear and belief that one's own human rights will be taken away. Understanding rights are not available worldwide, by any means, to everyone. In lower timelines and dimensions these patterns play out. Higher timelines are available now and a decision can be made to effect change for humanity. ~ **Archangel Gabriel***

Where Is Your Focus?

Fear bounces around even in the most grounded person. Redouble your efforts to bring about higher change to focus on clearing fear from your own energetic field and teach yourself to recognize when you are holding these emotional patterns.

Your "noise" adds to the collective. Refuse to add noise by mirroring love and authenticity out to neutralize free-floating fear and anger as this works to clear the continuation of polarity. Remember, people have been targeted for years for being different. This has developed fear of the "other."

*Dearest, we understand you are balancing speaking up with speaking out. This challenges you. A simple sentence saying, 'thanks for your input' and then moving on will help. This can increase your strength. Do not engage or block, as it also doesn't help. So, choose your sentence wisely. Thank you for your perspective. Personally, I choose to observe others' paths as I have enough on my own plate right now. Do this without comparing. Release and let it go as this is personal. ~ **Holy Mother Mary, Universal Angel***

*People project on each other. Empaths feel this and it becomes perceived weight, pain and a clogged brain. Some are fighting mad at life as they see it as penurious and harsh. This projection enters as a barb or saboteur weapon of peace destruction. Release that part of you and stand up like a lion. Roar, feels great, doesn't it? Speak up in a loving way. ~ **Lord Kumeka, Chohan of The Blue Ray***

*Dearest, attend to our energy. You will also feel the opposite energy arriving at the same time right now. It is sent by a darker agenda; it is no match for the light from the Central Sun. However, humanity will feel all of it. ~ **Blue Star Beings***

The Mother Wound

In April 2023, I taught a class called, "Universal Mothers" and together. We worked with understanding the Mother Wound that we all have within us.

We took a journey with coding to look at the lack of mothering or nurturing given to us in a loving, maternal way. We looked at ourselves to find out if we had a lack of attention or support in a way that we needed growing up.

We recognized that we may have felt as if we had to shield our mother or be her parent. We may have felt unloved or not loved as much as others in the family. We tried to please and show up as lovable. The consequence of this situation can cause us to act out or close up and not process our feelings.

When we grow up with this type of wound, addictions may develop, and we may find ourselves in abusive relationships. We can become a caretaker and over focus on others' problems and not our own. We feel fearful, insecure, unsafe, shameful, stuck, and we may have difficulty making decisions.

In class we worked on how to take our own needs seriously and set boundaries. We must learn to speak up and love our child within.

Often, when this is an issue, I will see a symbol of the client's breath being held and their throat chakra blocked.

This behavior is unconsciously waiting for the next shoe to drop.

Working on the mother wound and healing your inner child is one of the most important gifts you can give yourself. Then returning again and again to peace and having the understanding that, no matter what happens in your day-to-day life, you now have tools to bring yourself back to peace, to zero point. And in this focus on the moment, the future is just not a priority.

CHAPTER 5

Joy and the Heart Portal

Get your mind on joy and peace for your heart's sake. This small action brings you to your own zero point. We have a choice in every moment to decide whether or not we stay grounded, joyful, and observe or just react to what is around us. Many times, there is absolutely nothing to do!

Becoming watchful of our own programming is vital. Holding the mind in an open and curious state instead of claiming and labeling ourselves is the practice. The moment we say I am… something, I am "this thing," we take on that energy. Accept what is happening and solutions will show up.

Remember, your guides are always with you as Nostradamus reminds us here:

We of the New Earth wish to welcome all of you. A bright, shining new day is upon us. Precision work done by many of us partnering with you has allowed the new energy flow to be felt easily. Imagine walking to a river. You can hear the water trickling along; you can sense the elemental draw and a fullness of peace ahead even if your eyes are covered. Gnats, like small, irritating diversions can cause you to be distracted. Instead of reacting, do not waste your time. Come back into your heart. You can simply walk through the clamor of wings, knowing you will soon be placing your feet where you're meant to be, a destination of divine freedom. Your decision was made, your intention was heard. Keep going, you are almost there. ~ **Nostradamus**

We have heard messages of "soon" coming about New Earth for years! Depending upon how long you have been awakened and remembering, you may have heard channels saying that soon we will reach 5D. Many never spoke of 4D at all, but there is so much to learn in that frequency! We now truly understand that 5D is a frequency and not a 'place,' and that often we are adjusting our frequencies many times a day.

Here is an example: you've just come out of a meditation, and you are sitting peacefully on the sofa. You have a warm glow, and you feel calm and relaxed.

You notice that your dog is now on the floor, right there on the rug in front of you. During the meditation, when you were journeying and having such a wonderful time in the higher dimensions, now here you are back squarely into the 3-D when you notice the pup has made a little mess for you. Life happens! We still must answer to the physics of 3D. My friend Beth calls this burning up on re-entry!

Notice what dimension you are in by noticing your thoughts. When you recognize you are thinking negatively, stop and ground. Watch your words! A lovely 5D glow can morph into 3D in seconds! If you keep your thoughts and words as sterling as possible, you'll notice that life runs smoother. No need to judge yourself; ground and begin again.

The Holy Ones are speaking below about taking energetic responsibility:

All on planet Earth shall see a great unveiling. It will not do to become unhinged though many will. Self-possession is the watchword. Those who are still and observe shall then need to release the visuals and the noise around them. How is that accomplished, you ask? Know that to observe is to stand at the corner and watch the parade. But you will still hear the clamor, no? This friction is the rub! Really, it's so simple. Choose the parade you wish to view up close. Join in, if you will. But remember, there are consequences to your choices. Sometimes it's better to sit on the sideline two streets over. Perhaps the sunny side of the street is where you belong. There is nothing you can do to limit the noise, but it helps to watch from over on the peaceful side of the street. ~ **Benjamin Franklin**

Progress! Enough of you spoke up. War is close and over at the same time. There is a new frequency. Is it a new planet? Wait and see—you must have your own experience. ~ **Nikola Tesla**

The human resists, Soul. Surrendering in love with one's whole heart is the elusive step. The brain becomes open to change in ease then. One may then be present to Source. Kindly remind all to stand in love, be love, and be in love; and then surrender. Your own vibration makes the situation fall in your favor. So when you take responsibility to work on yourself, your vibration adjusts and your world falls into place. Your ego is the only thing in the way. ~ **Nione, Arcturian**

Do not think another moment about limiting your light. Opinions are swinging wildly right now on Earth. Are all of them valid? To the person opining, it feels as if their heart will burst if they hold their words in. Each must open up, make mistakes and stand up for their beliefs within a position of peace. Fear is a limiting choice, holding words in. Open your throat and heart and release what you need to say. ~ **Archangel Gabriel**

Reaching Out

Are you lonely? Are you missing someone? Reaching out even for a quick conversation can keep us connected and feeling like we have a lifeline.

My dear, change is afoot. People shall find that they miss others if they haven't realized it yet! Maybe it's time to reach out to those that cross your mind. Just ask the simple question, "How are you?" Then be truly interested! People are lonely and some fear being brushed off or closely questioned. It's exhausting to keep up with the pressure of the day and so many sit alone. It's my terrestrial birthday, so reaching out is the way I'd like people to honor me. It would be a heart blessing from one person to another. Social change starts with one person and an idea. ~ **Reverend Dr. Martin Luther King, 17 January 2022**

*Love flows constantly towards you. Revel in it. Do not look back! Break the habit of looking into the past. You know the past can be a trap. The only way is forward. Those who did not continue the journey with you have their own journey. Remember that if you still hold pain from the past, on this day, let them go in peace. Take it as your job today to release all who hurt you in the stream of peace available today. May God hold you as you do this. ~ **NikolaTesla***

Your Heart Portal

There are 33 chambers in the heart. Do we open our hearts only to a few and only to the people like us? No, we open up to all humans and all realms. What has held your heart hostage? It is true freedom to wake up and not have a single thing on the table to apologize for or anyone in our life holding something over us! It is time to step out of the control story and keep looking until you can see the elephant hiding in the bamboo.

*Suppose you are a truth teller, meaning you live your life openly and speak words that match it. But what if the words have no action behind them? Then what good is truth? Do you wait for the last breath to say 'This is what I believe in! I really meant to agree!' and say it in your last gasp? Without action words are just added noise to the already noisy. After this moment, ask yourself what action you will bring to the table, because the time for action is now. If you haven't learned about your heart for all that it is, then begin by knowing that it is a true doorway, a portal. Accept that it will take you everywhere you want to go. ~ **Benjamin Franklin on Standing One's Ground for Truth in Action***

Choose Yourself Over and Over Each Day

Because of your soul contract and agreements, patterns may show up as the saving and rescuing of your family members. You may have been the one separated out from the family and labeled as an instigator, a crybaby, and the black sheep. Maybe you were overlooked and unseen. Did you try to help? Did you focus on what you could do to get them to understand you? Did it eventually cause you to silence yourself? Did you ultimately become sick and exhausted? You may have felt stuck, frozen, suicidal, grieving, alone, or abandoned.

There is an opportunity to look at an old pattern when we are triggered during a harder time. This is where we make a concerted effort to build discipline into our practices. We will recognize that we are growing as we use the tools that we have learned for each situation that arises.

If you can recognize that you've been triggered, accept that this has happened, celebrate that you recognized it, and begin to work your magic.

Family Legends

It is a given that people, when ready, can see the patterns of behavior throughout the family going back generations—a family legend of choosing an abuser, for example, or alcoholism or drug abuse.

It can be more difficult to see that at the time. We might also choose someone to love whose behavior is similar to what we are used to. We didn't like it, but it was familiar. Then we go forward into the pattern of saving and rescuing.

As we maintain our practices daily and begin to choose our wellbeing and health, making it a priority, we recognize that there will always be hard times. But now we have tools, and we are able to pair them with gratitude since there is always something to be grateful for, isn't there? If you are beginning to recognize your family patterns and see yourself within them, congratulations on doing this important work.

CHAPTER 6

The Language of The Soul and Healing with Sound

*Music is the medicine of the soul. ~ **Seraphim Angel, Seraphiel***

Toning

I became a sound healer in February 2023 after I received my first guide, Juan, to assist me.

I am Juan, I come as a voice activation guide for you. First of all, rest with me and listen. Know the toning and your next new language is coming right on time. We wish you to practice each day.

There are activations and devices coming. You were part of a Mongolian family for two lifetimes. You are called to remember. You shall travel there in mind and heart. The golden eagle is also from me. You are transitioning into a new level. Your voice is now ready. Try it and add this device. This shall help the discomfort as you grow. We wish you to know there is so much more.

Sound added to any type of healing helps the energy to pass through a blockage easier. When you target specifically with intention, the block clears. Yes, it is a practice. You shall speak and sing more languages depending on the people in front of you.

The device feels like a golden disc in my throat. I practiced toning early on without calling in Juan or using the device and now there is a world of difference when I prepare my voice with my guide and call in the golden disk.

Opening the throat chakra

Many of us couldn't speak freely without consequences. Often, the louder more strident voice overran us.

There were seven lifetimes in this connection. Follow the threads and ask the guides to bring in the light. See the threads fall with ease. Send the entreaty to the souls now. Retract the threads that were yours and see them all away and disintegrate. See the violet and the golden light clear it. Give your thanks and the Ho'oponopono *for the freedom between souls. This has occurred. Power was the question, who had it? The power was in the silence and the inability to speak up. This caused a loss of power. Understand that anger and loss of control was in the family dynamic. ~ **13 November 2022, Debbie O'Connor, Beyond Quantum Healing Session for Me***

Speaking Up

Speaking up is often a hard-won lesson. Maybe we spoke up loudly and with harsh words at the beginning of saying what we needed to say. Know that working with the return of your voice might start with what you needed to say from the very beginning, and so the words will contain pressure. Often it is like starting up an old lawnmower. We sputter and strain and cough, and then finally the motor starts! Then we might blow out a bunch of black smoke. No matter how you start, keep going! Trust, because this becomes easier. Once we realize that regularly speaking up right at the beginning of a situation keeps the buildup from occurring. Our voice is then available to us when we need it, and our throat chakras are able to remain clear. This takes regular maintenance.

If I wake up with a sore throat, my first thought is to tone through it. This really works. You can begin by humming and looking for where that makes a difference in the body. Make the intention to hum to clear up the throat, or cough or anything you'd like to work in the body. Call in your guides for sound healing.

Begin to hum. Notice where your tongue is in your mouth. Moving your tongue can make your humming more interesting. Make a pop with your lips.

Then open your lips and tone the alphabet. Try it out! I often begin to hum, tone, and sing without calling in my guides first thing. I do that for a moment and then I call in my guides. Then I look at my throat itself clairvoyantly and make sure it's nice and clear. I clear my throat chakra with a chime bar. Then I hum, tone, and sing again. There is a marked difference before and after clearing.

My throat toning didn't really sound like anybody else's. I wouldn't have called it beautiful, musical, or something I could recognize as healing, except by me. I was feeling much better! Then I discovered the band called, "The Hu" on YouTube. Now I could understand my visions of arid landscapes and hunting, family, and the sounds that I finally knew as Mongolian.

From that point, I moved onto toning the Om and clearing chakras with the Bija mantras. You can find these sounds on YouTube and follow along. Speaking soul languages or light language, is something that you can also find many examples on YouTube.

My friend, Lola Singer, light language expert and artist, has her drumming circle and sound groups hold an intention before toning. Then she sings light language for that particular intention. She speaks many types of light language. Once you are familiar with different types—dragon, elemental, or Galactic, for example—you can pick out the type of light language or soul language people are speaking.

Soul language is meant to evoke a feeling or bring in healing, peace, and a rise in frequency.

Some sound healers use hand mudras, or they move their body in certain ways to bring in the energy or change it.

As we begin to explore our spirituality, we go through many changes. I prefer to call them initiations. The spiritual path requires us to take a deep look at ourselves in order to shed old beliefs and societal 'norms' that have been ingrained in us. We let go of concepts of who we once thought we were, face our deepest fears, learn forgiveness, raise our vibrations and begin anew.

A natural part of these initiations is waking up spiritual 'gifts' that we either suppressed or simply had no idea we ever had. For me, this was light language.

My journey began with the realization that my life was no longer fulfilling. I desperately needed a change, so I made the commitment to meditate every night when I got home from the job that I hated.

Meditation taught me to relax and to go with the flow so one night, when my hands started moving without me consciously controlling them, I amazed myself by watching my fingers form intricate patterns which I later found out are called 'mudras'. Mudras can be used to control energy and channel it to specific areas of our bodies for optimal health. I didn't know that at the time but I could definitely feel the good vibes clearing out the old stagnant energy and bringing in revitalized energy with every movement of my hands.

As I continued my commitment to meditate regularly, sounds began to accompany the mudras being formed by my hands. It was a very natural process that started with toning. I could feel the energy shifting within my body and raising my energy levels with each new tone I emitted. Over time, the tones gently evolved into humming, then consonant sounds, and eventually words which I did not recognize but that I knew felt good to my body. I had unlocked my gift of light language!

For those of you who are unfamiliar with light language, I like to describe it as your soul expressing itself through sound. Think of it as "language before there was language". There is no need to try to translate it because it is meant to be felt with the heart, not analyzed by the mind. Once that gift is unlocked, it purifies your body and harmonizes your energetic field.

The most important thing I learned about light language is that, like any spiritual gift, it needs to be used responsibly. That means we need to use it with INTENTION for it to be most helpful to ourselves and to others.

When I first started singing in light language, I sang and sang and sang ... and sang. It felt good in my body, and I would simply break out into song without giving it any thought.

Several spiritual mentors warned me that to use light language responsibly, I couldn't simply be scattering sound around. They explained to me that anybody or anything could scoop up that energy and use it if I didn't set an intention of where I wanted that energy to flow. I didn't like the idea of energy vampires or lower vibrational beings using my healing vibes for questionable purposes, so setting an intention for how the frequencies I create are being utilized became my number one priority. If you speak, sing, dance, or draw in light language, I encourage you to do so as well.

I have been speaking and singing in light language for more than ten years now. Setting the intention to heal the planet, help an individual, or aid the human collective gives light language a destination to flow to. Instead of scattering healing frequencies around haphazardly, these intentions create paths that are straight as an arrow and hit the mark.

When it comes to intentions, anything goes, so please make responsible choices.

As long as you set intentions that lead to expansion and benefit life, light language will flow where it is directed to go by you in the best ways possible.

If you sing, dance, speak or draw in light language the most powerful way to use it is to set an intention, direct the flow of the energy you are channeling, and trust that it is working. Relax and let the magic unfold (Lola Singer, personal communication, 2024).

Summer Solstice Ceremonies

I have been lucky to be a part of summer solstice ceremonies at Deb and Bruce Clements' house.

They live on a gorgeous property in Washington State filled with huge trees and places to gather. There's always a beautiful potluck feast when they invite us to come together to share time with our soul family. Everybody looks forward to the ceremony and the walk through the trails to get down to the altar. Every year there has been something new and different created by Bruce to notice on the path; a woven branch portal to walk through and special signs along the path by the little creek. We were surprised to see fresh cougar tracks on the path a few years ago when we returned back to the house after the ceremony!

Photos show the elemental kingdom and Native American influence on this beautiful place. Even with my naked eye I could see the many faces of the Little People in an area of tall grass.

Bruce said that for some reason he just didn't want to mow that big patch of grass. Many of us sang or spoke light language as an offering to the land last year.

The Great Eclipse

During the total solar eclipse on April 8, 2024, I asked my guide how to best support my energy, personal grid, and the Earth on that day.

Remember to speak up with a loud voice full of gratitude at this special moment. Call in the 4 directions.
Drum, sing, pray and focus upon the Earth and its waterways.
Listen to Earth and Nature.
Bring the stars into your prayers as you are Star and Stone.
Give gratitude for the time in between.
Put your feet into the ground.
Do not listen to fear. Listen to your heart.
What else is there? ~ **Chief Sitting Bull, Hunkpapa Lakota, South Dakota**

I was led to define my mission. You may have felt or heard the same words. I bring it in easily in divine timing and divine right order. There is no need to push or to fear.

CHAPTER 7

Mother Earth, Inner Earth and New Earth

*You must be grounded prior to flight. My child of the Moon and Stars, feel now my grounding presence. I am always with you. Calming waters come after the harshest storms. Trust in your own strength now to make good choices. No choice made from fear is as strong as a choice considered and then trusted. Remember, a wrong step is still a step forward. Forgive what you believe you did, or didn't do, because those were times of learning. Celebrate even the smallest forward motion. What others do now is no account for you and means nothing. Focus on yourself right now. ~ **Mother Gaia***

*A walk of holding space or standing in place as a witness is all that is required now. You are a witness of the construction after the destruction of the planet. It is truly revolutionary. ~ **Archangel Gabriel***

For those of us who work for this planet and spend time praying for peace, Mother Earth, is a sacred living being.

Nature, too, is a living energy that we can tap into. Her power, brought into a ceremony, brings another level to add to our prayer and energy work.

There is no denying it when you stand at the edge of the Badlands or on the sand near the Pacific Ocean or within the trees on Mount Shasta. Listen to the voice of Mother Gaia. She speaks with the wind, and she will meet you in Nature and Inner Earth.

Inner Earth

Many of us knew that mountains, under and inside the pyramids that are all around the world, are frequency devices, portals, and healing chambers that can heal the human and the land. We can feel this offering when we attune with the inner Earth or seek passage within the big trees, the mountains, and rock formations.

The mountains, the pyramids, and the trees scattered around Earth and, just like we human light bringers, hold the frequency to heal and to bring in this great awakening.

Many of my classes in 2022 and 2023 lead us inside and under, through tunnels to large, cavernous rooms at sacred sites all over the world using sacred geometry that is in tune with what is within us as humans. There, we met our guides through our higher selves.

We went to healing chambers and platforms for energy adjustment. We understood that we are all a little "planet Earth." We understood that, together, we can clear long-held energetic blockages in us and on and beneath the land.

All over the Earth, there are frequency holders, grid rebuilders and people, either by themselves or within groups, that took it upon themselves to work for humanity and the planet. We sat in meditation joined together in the high frequency areas on Earth to understand and work with the information there.

As my daily visualizations continue to change, I can see the advancement and work with my guidance team to understand the progress of humanity and Earth. There are ever-changing colors and symbols to chart progress.

I am happy to report there has been great change! Even more signs will appear and be easier to see. Take notice. The heavenly bodies, planet Earth, the sea, and all in-between wish to be noticed. It is time for all and everything to speak up and be heard.

New Earth

What happened? Did you feel it?

The Sun's energy and the flow of the plasma light to earth increases, a solar maximum is currently happening. This will offer change that looks like progress to some and destruction to others. The increase of light coming into the human vessel is not finished by any means. Resistance causes prolonged physical and mental discomfort. It doesn't stop the light—there will be light flashes. This is Earth's turn for great growth. Be a part of it by welcoming it in.

I have been viewing New Earth for years from a distance to get a good look at its development. In the beginning, I would see color changes. This developed into crystal which developed into crystal cities, and so on, until now I see New Earth as a living place full of people. I check out our planet regularly, too. Clairvoyantly, I look for color changes and energetic changes and other symbols. I see a little movie of all of it these days! This is helpful to understand what is going on with the planet and us humans.

The Golden Hours

*In this glorious Sirian Stargate, open up to the blue light above and below you and rest in its expansion as you are an amazing light yourself. Allow in this frequency of growth and healing. Feel Earth under your feet; see and imagine a golden light emitting upwards, allow it in and up through the body. Feel the turning as your body accepts this loving gift. ~ **Commander Ashtar, July 2023***

"You are witnessing a volcanic eruption that was something quite different. A higher system collaborated with nature; it was an end in timing to create expansion on several levels. Many were contracted to be affected by death and destruction for an agreed upon higher goal. Located along the path is a destination of the explosion/implosion. This occurred for humanity in macro. No one came away untouched. This event was simply one in the acceleration of planet Earth and must be viewed in a higher way. Occasionally, a match flame brings forth a desired result."
~ Nikola Tesla

I then heard the people's cry of "We still stand!" after devastating fire, floods, and volcanic eruptions.

It is hard to imagine something good coming out of these natural disasters. So, we stand in observation, and we pray for the highest results in divine timing.

The Golden Rebirth of Earth

It is nigh time to talk about the business of peace. The two are not mutually exclusive. It is the perfect time for rebirth. Now is not the time for citizens to bow under pressure but time to organize and structure as the days of creativity are upon you. ~ Abraham Lincoln

War is interesting to study, but as a frequency, it fractures. Watch for the cracks to appear, like oil and water, they are old foes. Be prepared for losses and gains as you all join in as Earth's protectors. Freedom is possible. Do not listen to doomsayers. ~ Nikola Tesla

Doomsayers are rampant. It comes from misreading signs. This type of speaking happens when fear is at the bottom line. The latest games of war have been considered and honed by the dark for generations. We are in the last days of force. Power can be seen coming to light worldwide. Stay in your powerful peace; let it flow as this is the truth. Be that reflection for the others in the way of the war machine. It does not exist only in war-torn places. Focus is put on the heads of war, but they are not the true architects, only a cover, so to speak. When the many become the mighty, the real picture of who controls whom becomes clear. The curtains fall now, do not look away. ~ Nostradamus

What is in a Cloud?

Our human brains search for patterns. A clairvoyant follows symbols to understand what they observe. Wikipedia describes Pareidolia as seeing faces or patterns in inanimate objects.

It is so much easier now to find the "Hello!" in a photo. Realms show up to give us messages. Keep looking! Keep paying attention to signs all around you in Nature and photos.

We are here. Last night was an event. You did not miss it. Do you recall it at all? No, this is for a simple reason; we are supporting your physical body. When your body is sufficiently prepared as your mind and emotions are prepared, you will then receive us in the physical sense. This time is drawing closer. Your instinct to purge is correct. Your dream is prophetic, but no harm shall come to us as you worry. Remember, worrying helps nothing and harms you. You had a good bit of it last night. You felt us draw in and the body felt the ship's energy. You all have served well on this trip. As you surmise, you are not finished as the cleanup continues. ~ **Commander Ashtar, Utah, June 2021**

Inner Earth Vision of the Telosians.

My vision of the Telosians of Inner Earth came to me when I was getting ready for sleep while camping on Mt. Shasta. This vision lasted about fifteen minutes as I was in the presence of a room full of beings of light. I felt their calm presence. They appeared human, but their limbs were tanned and long, and they resembled a big family.

Several years earlier, I found my way to Inner Earth nearby on Bunny Flat on Mt. Shasta.

I found the opening for Inner Earth right in front of me as I worried, I would not find it, and was looking and thinking way too hard! I went through the tree and down into Earth where I met with Mother Gaia. I have been back to visit her and bring people there many, many times since.

Just ask and say, "Show me!" then open your heart and you will see the magic that is available to you.

The Blue Column of Celestial Support, *Blue Star Beings*:

The Blue Beings showed me their column of light that comes down from the galaxy from Sirius star and flows over the Earth and into Inner Earth. I was advised to begin to use the column in every opening for journeying, healing, and meditation.

When working with the blue column as part of the four directions, I sense an easy rise and grounding at the same time.

This is easy for my clients and students to imagine. If further grounding is needed, we go down into Earth in our vision and put our cords or our feet in the blue dirt. Grounding and reunification practices change often, as we humans are developing. It is so exciting being here on the Earth now! This is what we came for, the ascension cannot be denied.

CHAPTER 8

What in the World is Around Us?
The Grids and the Realms

The Crystal Grid

The 6D selenite expanse is visualized on the walk to the selenite bowl over the golden crystal grid, my symbol of zero point. This is called in during every reading and class. It is a part of grounding and reunification with the AOYE work.

When we step up onto the grid during meditation, we listen for the Earth's gentle hum as our crystalline body tunes to the grid below our feet and relaxes. We re-tune when we are standing on this dimensional pathway.

Each second our planet becomes new. You too have the ability to become new and flexible within each moment, even during the harder times.

Get to know your own crystal grid in your meditation spot or your own yard. Imagine it as part of your armoring. Within the four directions this crystal grid can take you to other dimensions.

Using protection or armoring for your energetic field – it is up to you, along with whatever level you wish to use. Most people I know do at least some armoring every day. It's important to keep your energetic field healthy, and this will help. My armoring has adjusted to something quite different than in the past as it is easier now to see and sense incoming energy and adjust in the moment. Getting used to how you feel in the body and paying attention to energetic changes allows you to act right away. Clearing your field at the moment of attachment is so much easier than living with it for hours or days. Remember you have free will. Use your free will to move along any energy that has a lower frequency than you do.

If you challenge yourself, you shall see that your dream can be bigger. ~ ***Archangel Michael of the Sun***

I come today to assist the imagination. As you know, that is the beginning. ~ ***Ascended Master Jesus Christ***

Stepping into My Power and Releasing Entities

We moved from Washington State to Pennsylvania in July of 2023. We found a temporary residence to stay in while we looked for a house.

As soon as we arrived, I began to notice there was a whirlwind of spirit activity in the neighborhood. Saint Francis told me that my temporary residence is part of an old house in Lancaster City and was a practice space to bring in the light. He reminded me to shine as bright as possible and balance my energy. I had to learn to stand up for myself in a new and more powerful way.

We experienced challenge after challenge during that eight-week period. The energy around the neighborhood was dense with entities, trapped, deceased, and emotions. When I noticed my dogs were feeling the energetic hits, I said I was done with allowing this activity in my backyard. Clearing my space is a regular part of my day but being tired after a trip across eight states, and getting used to the heat and humidity, had taken its toll. This activity level was higher than I was used to.

We were lucky to find that place to rent. We met lovely people and had a great time walking around and seeing all of the old colorful buildings. Once we were situated and going out to look for houses, we knew we made the right choice to move to Pennsylvania.

It is always our choice to say yes or no. The lion is meant to rear up on her hind legs sometimes and say, "No more, not me, not now, and not ever!" Freedom exists in that declaration.

"I have freewill, and this is my space. All leave now, go back to Source!"

I took time to clear our little space to a much higher and brighter level, and I included the block around the apartment. Then I flowed the Violet Flame for over a mile away.

Almost instantly, there was a noticeable difference. I could then see clearly high above our backyard, and I noticed all of the elementals and angelic guides that had come to assist. The dogs relaxed and we were all able to enjoy the rest of our stay.

A Visitation, Tacoma, WA

In the afternoon of 17 January 2023, I took my dogs out onto the back porch. It was raining. We all stood for a minute together. They don't like to get their feet wet even if they need to go outside and do their business.

I walked to the edge of the left side of the porch just under our metal roof and I looked up into the sky. Between the lilac bush and fence, coming in low and straight at me, was a hawk with mostly white and some brown feathers. Not more than eight feet over my head, his eyes were on mine. His wingspan was wide. At the last second, he pulled up.

I turned to make sure the dogs were still on the porch with me. They were, so I went off of the porch and looked around, scanned up and over the roof. I looked in all directions for the hawk. He was nowhere.

The dogs stood on the porch, curiously calm.

I was able to understand through channeling that this was a vision from Chief White Hawk.

The hawk has always meant prosperity for me, and he had a message about the future.

More and more I was receiving messages that it was time to move on. My work was done on the West Coast.

*Look to the horizon, not on the ground in front of you. Give respect to the Avians. This is requested for further attention for our assistance in the passing of messages of peace along with the trees over the entire world. ~ **Channeling from the Bird Nation and Small Realm of Bugs and Insect***

There are natural energetic devices scattered all over the Earth. For example, in the Western United States there is Bear Lodge or Devil's Tower, Mount Shasta, Mount Hood and so many more. There are portals, grids and ley lines connecting sacred sites.

*You are feeling the nearness of the crafts now. The dial is turned up and the frequency is felt from heavenly bodies, the Moon and other planets. Expect more of what you witnessed today. All are observed in peace, as anything else just makes the physical fluctuations uncomfortable. Hold your grid point and ground. This is why many people feel like staying home. You are meant to rest at this time. ~ **Commander Ashtar, Lions Gate 2023***

*Listen now, attend. We will speak as one after today. We are your aspects and as part of you, we asked for the consideration of time spent speaking together. Call us forward and we shall do this today. ~ **Herve, Lyran, Lions Gate 2023***

In late 2023, as we flowed into embodiment, aspects were returned back to me. I see this as a process that we may revisit. When we are ready, our mother's and father's lines return. We can ask to see where and when we lost pieces of our soul and return them back to us through the heart into wholeness again.

*I am here to pave the way. We know that you all have wanted to understand just how human action in assisting the realms work. We link through the mind and heart and a plan is made. This plan has been in creation. Finally, the efforts are showing up upon Earth for all to see. ~ **Pleiadian Guide***

*As such, the planet does not exist in the old way. Humanity still bobs in and out of several dimensions at a time. The change must occur within the human. Our star brothers and sisters are here and their energy adds to the otherworldly feeling. Some people believe in this ascension, they feel it and they believe. Some can imagine it and some do not believe in it at all. It will be this way going forward for a while. There will be vast opportunities to share regarding this, but people will allow themselves to awaken when it is time for them. It is always one's free will. ~ **Chief Sealth, Duwamish and Suquamish, Washington State, Lions Gate 2023***

*The Sun rises. The Sun sets and in between, life. Those who wish to see a bigger picture shall see it. Many won't, it will be as if nothing has happened. Remember, you shall be ready. ~ **Mother Africa***

There will be people who will not feel the ascension. They may just understand their daily life has begun to feel a bit easier. Or they might feel a push to change. There are people on the Earth now that are here at this time to be mirrors and not be part of the ascension. There are people on this planet who hold the energy.

Right or wrong is not the focus, the walk is the focus. And when a decision is made, one can walk forward. It is a yes or no that brings peace. When one is on the fence the energy is insecure. It is no real choice. ~ **Entirah Meh, Syrian Council of Light**

The Council of Nine, 2023

This multi-realm counsel is a group of guides that I have worked with for years, sometimes visiting singly. They tell me that the power of a group of souls concerned to a particular soul, question, or situation will increase the size or ability of the concern to clear. They tell me they are with me now to increase my soul's experience, the growth of the groups with whom I work, and the quickness of all endeavors.

At this moment, it is imperative to limit your ongoing behavior of future thinking, worry and looping. This is achieved by less screen time, increased alone time, rest, and simple activities. This will all make sense as you do it. The speed of your daily activities must slow down. The speed of the outer world may continue to feel faster and more chaotic. These things are entirely up to you. Once done and a habit is formed, your day shall continue to contain these behaviors. Exercise, stretching, meditation, rest and a small act of simple pleasure, such as drawing or coloring, painting or art of any kind, getting outdoors and grounding and preparing nourishing meals will go a long way towards peace.

You are learning about your new role on Earth. This will be a full embodiment. Trust all is well. This was not a "walk in" situation in the way you perceive it. More of you will be returning in the full expression of embodiment. Most shall embody depending on their roles going forward. ~ **Entirah Meh, Sirian Council of Light**

Mary No Face

Heyokas, Sacred Clowns

Who am I? Eventually we all ask ourselves this question. The Root Council helped me to remember my name.

Those who love us, sit with us at the fire and feed us. They remember us for who we are. They hold each other close as they are true brothers and sisters. Humanity will remember this. Just as the sun rises each day, there are constants. Why does it take so long to remember? The Sun remembers effortlessly. The human brain has agendas and forgets to rest. Even the Sun rests. ~ **Chief Sitting Bull, Hunkpapa Lakota, South Dakota**

Life is stretched out before you. How you use the time you are allotted is up to you. This is the key to life. It all comes in timing. Remember, power looks at the snake in the face and sees an ally, not a thing to fear. This is power versus force at its essence. When one asks Fear its real name; things change! Sometimes labels deceive. What is a friend can be a foe and the reverse is also true. What is the snake's name? Fear can instead be knowledge. Use it well, Seeker. ~ **Chief Red Cloud, Oglala Lakota, South Dakota**

The Land, Our Heart

*Today's vision is a connecting one as you are now part of the four directions themselves. The four sectioned heart that you have been seeing represents Earth, Air, Fire, Water and so much more that you cannot see yet. ~ **White Buffalo Calf Woman, Lakota, South Dakota***

Worldwide events

*Remind all Seekers of the potency of group focus. Simply to love and to direct a path forward as one step forward at a time adds up. ~ **Saint Joseph***

*There have been many recent events that have impacted the world. The true causes have not been revealed, and they may never be. Many can be settled by the seventh ray, the Violet Flame. Many souls have contracted to be part of these devastating events. The events worldwide from this moment on shall mean more to humanity once seen clearly. Be vigilant in what you support. Your thoughts must stay focused on peaceful resolution. The time is now to walk the talk. Be ever mindful of listening to what is hidden under the words of people 'in the know.' Listen through the heart only as the mind is still easily programmed and can be swayed. ~ **Nikola Tesla***

*Love is the answer, but why is love offered, now? The answer is that it can be given abundantly at any time. It is the gift that is always appropriate and combined with the power of many, can create open minds and miraculous results. ~ **Holy Mother Mary, Universal Angel***

The *Ho'oponopono*

My friend, Deb Clements and I drove from Tacoma to Hood River, Oregon in May 2022 to meet up with our friends at the Eceti Ranch. We were gathering to be a part of the weekend for night viewing of galactic ships that can be seen flying over the ranch. It is a peaceful place, a perfect spot to look over towards Mount Adams and watch the ships in the night sky.

It doesn't take long to recognize that what you are looking at is a star, a satellite and what is definitely a ship; especially when they "power up" and increase their glow or speed. There are lots of videos on YouTube in which one can see the ships over the ranch.

It's a pretty straight shot up I-5 to Hood River. Somewhere, we got creative and drove up a mountain road we weren't supposed to. There, we found a lot more snow than ever anticipated. We both believe that this little detour was divinely orchestrated. I've been to the ranch before. It felt like we were so close! We stopped to ask for directions. The address had an 11 in the name of the road. I got out and asked for directions at a barn near the ranch. Playing in the barn were eleven fluffy white puppies. A sign! We needed to have this detour. The energy going up that mountain was so beautiful. It turned out the next day we saw a sign and realized that we had been in the Gifford Pinchot National Forest and if we had been able to come all the way down, there was the perfect road leading right near the ranch. Snow got in the way, so we just turned back around.

Of course, we saw plenty of ships at night! There's a beautiful labyrinth on the property where I met one of my guides for the very first time! I came out of that meeting with my eyes wide open and my mouth, too! I kept saying he is so tall. I just couldn't get over it! You can't forget Commander Ashtar. As was in instances of meeting Master Jesus and others, many beings try tricks to make you think they are the being of light. Once you meet the real one and not an imposter, you will be able to easily tell someone who is trying to fool you with their lower vibration, wrong colors, and lower frequency message. Similar to an AI rendered drawing and one drawn by a living artist.

A Perfect Day for Freedom

They pulled the sheet off the Statue of Liberty. All shall see their own truth, as well as larger truths. We then will pull the emperor's clothes off and stand together, one people. What many don't see yet is to harm one is to harm all. Uncovering and viewing down to bare bones, as it is seen in death, allows all to understand a very simple truth. Uncovered and unvarnished, the reflection is the same. It can't help being so. The human heart comes to bare. As we observe our bones, and our blood and skin return, and we see just who we are and who we have always been, then blame, guilt, shame, pain, woe and misery will not exist within us anymore. When we become a pile of bones on the land, the rebuilding can take place. **~ Chief Sealth, Duwamish and Suquamish, Washington State and Chief East Lee, Lakota, Eagle Butte, South Dakota, speaking on a day important to the United States.**

Many are coming from the four corners. The black shroud is released. Lifetimes of being stolen, raped and killed, hence the symbol of the handprint on the face. It was not pleasant to feel, like all wounds we have suffered by this particular hand of greed, abuse and control. All fall in the false light. The ones who said, 'Let us take care of you, we know best.' But like cockroaches in the kitchen light, they scurry back to their hidey-hole when the bright light is shown. This time the hole is closed. There are groups such as the one you are a part of that speak up for a reason. Why would people congregate out of shared anger if there wasn't a trauma suffered in the first place? Peace can be learned. Right now, is a time where the world saw the result of hatred and many decided no, not me. Not anymore. When one chooses to heal, hatred and groups that stick together with the glue of shared trauma unravel. This is what you are noticing. Keep noticing. **~ Chief East Lee, Lakota, Eagle Butte, South Dakota**

Intend today to see the lightness of Earth. There are choices, clear ones. Make the choice to foster peace. Yes, some need the illusion of safety. Let them have it. It is no one's path to say what is true for all. **~ Ascended Master Jesus Christ**

I have had visions of galactic ships many times in my life. The small and large ships near the Eceti Ranch, triangle ships, and small Merkabah ships. But I distinctly heard a ship once, years and years ago, in a meditation in West Seattle. I heard the metal clank. I heard the sound of a buzz; I'd always heard galactic ships were silent. Maybe I just needed to pay attention! My friend, Kathleen, and I witnessed two ships—one in West Seattle and one in Tacoma, Washington. When I still lived in

Tacoma, we went for a walk on a windy day. We both saw a distinct cloud that absolutely was moving when everything else was still.

Open your heart and mind and you will be able to see all that is around you. The realms are so active, and you will get used to looking for signs while out for a walk or a drive.

CHAPTER 9

Crossing Souls and Going Home

*Dearest, you received what was meant to be noticed. Rest! Eat, pray. Look for signs. It is a perfect day for freedom. ~ **Grandfather Rainbow Medicine Man, Puyallup and Tulalip, Washington State: Grandfather was speaking to us about personal freedom on that early May morning.***

A Shaman's Journey: California, Arizona, Spain, and Pennsylvania

In late May 2021, I set out on a 17-day journey across six states with my friend, Melanie Long. Traveling by trailer, we had a loose goal and a few plans to head to Mt. Shasta and then on to Sedona, Arizona.

Almost instantly signs began to show us that this was not going to be just a road trip. A day or two down the road on our "vacation" we began to hear from other spiritual friends regarding what we were meant to do. Look for the signs they all said.

We began to understand that we would find areas needing our assistance to energetically clear the land and cross Indigenous trapped souls, and possibly others. With assistance from shamans and other healers across the country, we were to plan a ceremony every night.

We learned to watch for signs and markers to guide us on what to do that day. We met many representatives in spirit along the path. We spotted over 100 eagles, some golden eagles, on our journey and, once we came into Mount Shasta, we saw eagles every day. There was a very memorable evening that ended in meeting a beautiful mother skunk.

We joyfully ate Mexican food every time we could. We hugged and loved on the trees and rocks and sang to pass the time, hearing the song, *Achy Breaky Heart* quite a few times.

I spoke with my deceased mom, Vivian, near Mount Shasta on her birthday, June 4th. She told me to go back three generations to find my Native American heritage. She told me our guidance team will make markers known to us.

My mother in spirit pointed out that Melanie is a divine healing partner with me and since then, that truth has been validated over and over again. Melanie learned to drive her trailer rig on this trip. Looking back, I hope I was moral support. We had quite a few things go wrong, but we laughed at ourselves and learned a lot. Now, I understand that this trip was in preparation for a much bigger trip. Small things like getting used to the hot weather and little or big inconveniences were just lessons on the road. We found that we were easy travel companions and spent long hours looking at the day's photos and laughing together like kids.

My Notes, 4-6 June 2021

The weather has changed from 85° with clear blue skies to heavily chem-trailed skies; then dropped down to 40° at night on the mountain.

We saw four deer on the ridge that same morning, overlooking Mt. Shastina when we went to pray for the soul of someone who had just crossed over. We saw eagles every day. On my mother's heavenly birthday, we had the first ceremony. So many souls! We could see the women and children. I saw salmon in a vision, and they were coming out of my body when Chief Joseph healed me. So many shamans came in. We gave great thanks as we laid tobacco down. Melanie had a box of all we needed for the ceremony. Tonight, I saw a skunk on our walk back to the trailer. I've never seen a black and white skunk in real life before. In the morning, I saw a tall kachina along the road with a black and white face. I later saw dancers with black and white faces.

Symbolism? Absolutely!

Who, Me? An Unlikely Shaman

In 2021, on my mother's birthday on June 4th, I learned of my Native American family connection through my great grandmother. I later learned one can be born a shaman. I had to work to understand what it means to be a shaman as I was advised by my guides that it is a lifelong path. My cousins have stories of the connection, I would later learn.

If one is called to the shaman's path, do not take one moment of wonder if you are meant to do this. Pay close attention to those who are called to walk with you. Each one has a part. Ceremonies continue.
*~ **Archangel Gabriel 17 June 2021***

*We have been many times Indigenous as we travel back and forth between time. Look further. Feel into your heart for your connection to your great grandmother. This is the way. ~ **Chief Sealth, Duwamish and Suquamish, Washington State***

The Small Group consists of four people who work together with Indigenous Chiefs and medicine men and women of many tribes in Spirit. They are our guides who came here before us, working together with trapped souls who return back to Source. Those in spirit and those in body, working together, have power to show the way home. The souls of many came forward when they were ready to release extreme pain in the face of terrible acts of war and terror. Each one of us has a role, and we intend to do our part. These ceremonies were very emotional. Listen to the word of support from The Holy Ones as they help us to learn about what we are meant to do.

Use your voice and platform for love that is given along with an offering from the Celestial realm daily. We will meet you when your heart is open. We will be there when you are in fear and experiencing loss. Yes, the time is now. Open your eyes as all will be easier seen. Do not look away from the grief of others for your heart may be strengthened in the love of those around you who hold the frequency of *peace. Fear weakens. It is an attractor and a lighthouse for more fear, and the possibility of the mind and body to look at the truth but see a lie. ~ **Holy Mother Mary, Universal Angel***

*You both are assisting souls to cross, but they will not cross yet. Tonight is a night to listen to their anger and love that was lost so honor them and listen. Ask for a representative to shift the soul agreements. You must stop processing through your body. This absolutely must happen when you assist so many. ~ **Grandfather Rainbow, Medicine Man, Puyallup and Tulalip, Washington State, 5 June 2021***

*Dearest, hold no fear. Tonight, you shall see multitudes. Many souls and much anger here. Horror, disappointment, regret, and sadness, it is deep inside this dirt. This mountain is a witness to the cries of pain and loss, anguish, and fear. Do your best; it is time. ~ **Bavado, Blue Thunder, Shaman, Shoshone, Wyoming***

*You must make time for the dead and the suffering. You hold the key. Receive it now again. It holds divine power and is not meant as a trifling thing. Crossing souls in love is what you do. Use this key in your heart. A psychopomp's journey is not an easy one. It can be painful. Regular checkups of your own heart are needed as your light calls the suffering. ~ **Anubis***

As a psychopomp, we see and feel the needs of the dead. The dead are aware of us, too. The light in our hearts calls to them. The medium holds both love and neutrality when receiving their words and information. We always have the choice to assist their crossing, allowing them their own decision as to how and when it unfolds.

*On 25 December 2022, the Small Group crossed many hundred thousand. This has been a group effort with the Tribes, the Earth and Inner Earth. We have supported the land as you have. We wish to bring an offering back to the land. ~ **The Wanderer, Medicine Man, Tulalip, WA, 14 March 2024***

This beautiful being of light showed me what to do. I flowed the energy from the place I consider sacred, to my city and out to my state, then to the entire East Coast and back to the West Coast. I passed this energy throughout the United States.

The River of Life

I saw the soft yellow light draw me down to the living tree. I saw everyone who was supporting us in their own spot and my place began in a silent, still area of the softest yellow light. I followed my guides into a tunnel. I could see animals of all types passing by me. We all walked down to an Inner Earth Sea, far underground. There was a sea of light and water. As far as I could see in front of me, there was golden light. It was the true Rainbow Bridge beyond shining with every color in the world and beyond. There is a great draw to go home. This is why Archangel Michael stands in front of me when I assist souls to cross.

Drawing Boundaries (or Having Firm Business Hours)

The deceased and beings from other dimensions have reasons to bring a message through, but sometimes it is in our timing to learn good boundaries. The deceased who need help are insistent. You may be getting visits at all hours. I regularly make a statement that my time is my own and I do not appreciate being visited late at night. That said, depending on the energy of the soul, I may decide to stop and assist right then if I am not too tired. But remember, we all must draw a boundary as to when and who can contact us. No lower energy or entity is welcome in my home or sacred space. When I notice something has shown up, I take the time to clear up the energy immediately. Always ask for help if you need it. Make sure you ground and call in your own guides and ask for assistance.

If you need professional help, do not hesitate to call a psychopomp.

Calling in a Gatekeeper

It is up to you when, where, and whom you will receive. Calling in a gatekeeper to assist is an action that protects us from becoming overwhelmed. Adjust by setting a limit through your higher self as to how many souls at a time you will allow to come near you during mediumship. This gatekeeper should be a trusted person on the other side who will keep you safe and allow you the space to focus and remain grounded.

Through your higher self, you may make statements such as I am open to receive messages from souls through my gatekeeper. I am open to receiving messages from ascended masters, angels, galactic beings of light, Earth and Inner Earth beings, and so on. I am open to receiving symbols, signs, and colors as messages. Remember, signs and symbols are the way nature and other beings communicate with us.

How does it physically feel to bring through someone from the other side and be in the presence of a divine master, or higher being of light? You may feel tingly and notice pressure in your third eye, heart, or within your body entirely. Your energy may feel lifted or relaxed, or you may have a unique way of understanding just who is with you. These are your "tells," and you will learn to rely on them. This takes practice, and remember, practice is your greatest teacher.

Crossing Souls at the Campgrounds

It soon dawned on us that we were in service to those we would meet along this journey.

We met an elderly couple, newly married. On that beautiful California morning, we brought through the man's departed wife. This gave him great peace.

We met a huge dog that ate several steaks before anyone noticed. That dog looked miserable. We worked on him, and you could see a noticeable difference! The light came back in his eyes. Before we left for our next campground, the Pit Bull's dad gave us a present! We met many people and animals this way. Somehow, if you are in the right place, something will come up in conversation and you can be in service.

We had ceremonies at the campsites at night. Occasionally, people camping near us would join in. One night, we arrived very late at camp. It was dark and the time was coming close to when we were slated to connect up with the rest of the Small Group and other Shamans over the phone. The campground was confusing, and we couldn't find our spot. We saw a young Native American man in his car by the side of the road. I told him we were lost, and he jumped in his car and took us right to the place. I said we were late for ceremony! He was an angel, for sure.

Allowing the Stuck to Stay Where they are Stuck.

Some stuck souls are still in the process of witnessing and observing. It is their decision if and when they will cross over. The Small Group is a living being. Even if we are not physically together, speaking face-to-face, the work is still being done. These agreements were voiced prior to incarnation. They are still strong and unwavering. Life came to the forefront for each of us in the guise of illness, corruption, family worries, lessons, and it is all understood now as lessons for building the team.

Part of the Small Group's duty is to clear the Earth of the lower frequencies and assist in bringing in the new. We look and feel into the dark and the light and give our love in service. Our guides supported us every step of the way. We became in the habit of discussing with our guides each day what was on our mind. When questions come up, ask! That's how the Team knows you are ready to learn and in timing to do so.

You are feeling, more than ever, people's reactions when they are unable to hold their own frequency. This is true in life and within the land. Going forward, it becomes easier. True healing is anything and everything that is apart and then back together. Imagine a beaded belt. It can't be used or worn in two pieces, can it? But woven together again or redone, repaired and healed it then becomes useful and beautiful again. Not all will understand this idea. Some will say no, start over! But the old can be mended just as a hand reaches out from the past in love. ~ ***Chief Sealth, Duwamish and Suquamish, Washington State on What is True Healing***

You are struggling with a question only love will answer. Hand it over. It gets easier and the understanding of truest love shall commence. ~ ***Chief Sealth, Duwamish and Suquamish, Washington, State***

Today we meet again. We connect through the eye of the world. Together we work in the Small Group. Great Raptor speaks now and all listens. ~ ***Chief Willenawah, Great Eagle of Tellico Corn Tassel, Cherokee Nation:***

You are both hearing clearly. If one is not of your tribe or family, you are going backwards through the desert if you think they are. Be done and see what you get. ~ ***Chief Joseph, Nez Perce, Idaho, 11 June 2021***

The purpose is always love. There is no other. To die a good death is a privilege and not every heart gets the small favor. The struggle on Earth today is coming to an end. When the sky meets the Earth, the day has arrived. Until then there is only love. ~ ***Chief Crazy Horse, Oglala Sioux, South Dakota, 9 July 2022***

When I heard the message that the Sky had met the Earth in the summer of 2023, I knew the prophecy had come true.

The goal for The Small Group is to continue to support Earth's growth and the new dimensions. The release and homecoming of trapped Indigenous souls constitute a give-and-take of energy. The stagnant, trapped death energy and with it the cries of injustice and torture, pain, and fear when released, then transmutes. This is also a calling, an energetic exchange for when the souls are released, the new souls come forward. These returning souls are of a higher frequency that will add to the buoyancy of earth. The Chiefs are your guides. We also hold the frequency of change.
~ ***Enti Rah Me, Sirian***

The path is open, my dearest ones. Ask your feet to carry you along it in ease and strength, for that is true power that can make anything happen.

Imagine a well woven rope. It relies on the strands next to it, knowing all is woven in with the same intention, to be strong and of service, without constantly wondering why each strand is woven next to one another.

Constant belief, and with the sister next to you, as it is written in the stars, will show the path and it will be illuminated without worry.

May the Creator bless you. We wish to invite each of you to speak of your willingness to continue upon the path that has been laid out by this family of light. You are tired. Remember why we supported one another; we are a cohesive unit when we work together. This translates to being a cohesive unit in transmutation as well.

Clear yourself and you clear your sisters. Make the choice each day to focus upon your health as your group feels your successes. If you wish to continue the path after the season, we welcome you.

Quietude is important for all of you before the ceremony to hear us clearly as the dark hides in indistinct places. You've seen some of it, not all, but you are "slightly in the dark", as you do not realize the magnitude of souls to cross yet.

Each of you is learning to remember. You are loved, and small mistakes are for learning.

The Elemental and Nature realm truly assist endeavors of the group. All animals cross instantly and instantly return. You were seeing a true "ghost reenactment" so to speak.

Clearing the earth of the lower frequencies will assist in bringing in the new.

A healing shall render faster and, in many cases, instantly. This can be said for all layers in the web of life. The hand that reached out will be clasped by those willing to walk in through peace.

Remember, we are the keepers of the land.

What is true healing? Anything and everything that is apart is returned back together. ~ ***7 June 2021: Chief Sealth, Duwamish and Suquamish, Washington, State***

You four are one heart. Go forth, whether traveling in body or mind, and bring the prophecy home. Yes, the symbol of the white deer in your vision is The White Buffalo transformed. Now send the love out powerfully. ~ ***White Buffalo Calf Woman, Lakota, South Dakota:***

One sister is the physical representative of our own hearts. As she travels, please hold the image of the gold piece. Her worth to all of us is beyond price, and we wish to acknowledge altogether the Small Group's worth as well. If you have felt as though you are in stasis, know you are simply resting, and when we come together, you all will feel the true regeneration of this time. All is in perfect, divine and holy timing.

Do not dwell on the tiny worries of others or the day. All comes together, seamlessly.

*Behold the blue sky. It is blue in reality whether there are clouds present or not. The river flows forward, and we all follow. ~ **Chief Red Cloud, Oglala Lakota, South Dakota (speaking of one of the people in the group who was traveling while the rest of us stayed home)***

The Vision of The Tattered Flag Hung by One Corner
Channeled in Honor of the Lee Family

*The message, quietly stated, is a demand for peace and justice! There has been none yet. There, that is how I reflected force. Peace, love and freedom is an ideal some hold. Did I, could I, have held this in my Earthly lifetime? No, I believed in the ultimate force of death after loss, after loss and more loss again. Feel this for you all have had your losses, privileges taken, too, in different ways. The heart tunes to love, freedom, and the power of moving beyond the past, yet not forgetting, and honoring those we've lost to the horrors of violence. The flag shall fall, and it should. What rises is the open heart you have seen all week. ~ **Chief Sitting Bull, Hunkpapa Lakota, South Dakota***

*The group took on the energy of death, fear, grief and war. It may take a bit of time, but you shall be released of it. You all will eventually come to understand your need for better preparation. ~ **Chief Sealth, Duwamish and Suquamish, Washington State***

There is a feeling within the human body when a deceased soul is around or attached to our energetic field. In photos there is a distinct look to the living when there is discarnate energy around that person. There is a feeling, a true sense of bloating or heaviness. A camera can pick it up.

The psychopomp may feel pain or discomfort within the body, along with anxiety or other emotions. Clearing after a ceremony of crossing is imperative. Preparations prior to the work must be taken very seriously. Doing this work with a large number of souls crossing over makes caring for yourself a priority. I check to be sure I am free of all death energy afterwards and again the next day.

*We appreciate the group's efforts and lift you each up into the light of day. As morning broke, many of you felt the clearing of the storm inside you. To make sure that you use this last meeting as a guide, one must focus on what you felt, perceived, and heard during the ceremony. Your own clues were scent and emotion. Others had their own experience. ~ **Coyote, Medicine Man, Nez Perce, Idaho***

Lessons after lessons are placed before the soul for its growth. They are meant to be embraced, but at this time on Earth, many feel their problems are like a rainstorm without cease. This, too, is meant to be embraced.

There will soon be a time where the human will see why this epoch was so special, such a huge transition that one shall look back in wonder at all of what you came through.

It's not possible to see how the chains link up yet, though you try and you think you know. Ask yourself do you trust? If you do, you will know, deep in your heart that all trials are in place for the soul's growth.

Each new problem's lock has a key to it. Humans see patterns and can always see other's patterns in a clear way, so much better and easier than they can see their own!

*Now is the time to understand that there is always a further step. A healer assists with what they can see. What another person does with this information is up to that soul. Release yourself with that understanding because the problem is not yours. Balance in each is the key. The light shall enter every soul. There should be no more thought as to the light missing someone. ~ **Ascended Master Jesus Christ***

This is the comforting message that I received when my niece passed away.

*Dearest, your loved one has crossed into the loving arms of her mother. She shall need several days to acclimate as you know. Tell the family to hold easy space as now is the time for her reuniting with family and her creator. Trust now as a larger force pulls her into freedom. ~ **Ascended Master Jesus Christ***

Our dear girl, we visit you today. The Christ light abounds. We, too, are with her. No worries, as she will come to you soon. Tell our loved one (speaking of another family member) how much we love her and to rest in the peace of knowing that Creator God's promise abounds.

Faith in oneself is needed at this time. The Earth shall heal, and humanity shall come into the golden state that has been missing for so long.

*Rest well in the light of the promise, both of you, with our eternal love. ~ **My Mom and Dad***

El Camino de Santiago, Spain, October 2022

I was hired by Spain Adventures to spiritually assist a group of people walking the Camino de Santiago. My job was to channel information and give a voice for spirit guides to use as they show up along the way. Ahead of the trip, I began to listen to the guides who came forward.

*Peace upon you, dear ones. The path has been traveled successfully by seekers with the same questions since there has been a path! Should you go now? Why not? Walk forward with the Sun. It is the original protector, the first light of strength. Do you feel safe enough to let go? ~ **Saint Francis***

Prior to setting out on the Camino, Melanie and I stayed with our friend in Las Graneras, a beautiful, small village of 300 souls one mile off the Camino path. It was a perfect place to acclimate and get ready to meet the others who were coming a few days later.

Melanie and I suffered mishap after crazy mishap along the way and soon we realized all was in divine timing. I got locked in the bathroom on the train. We lost things. We had items taken from us at the airport. I was vigorously searched several times! Soon we caught on and had fun no matter what. By the time we had slept off a bit of jet lag, it was time to explore the beautiful little chapel in town.

The chapel felt like a portal to the past. In a vision I saw people fighting outside the doorway. I later had a very detailed vision of a mother and child.

After a few days, our little group again acclimated to becoming a bigger group of peregrinos. Below are early the channeled messages we received.

A hearty, welcome to your new adventure! A mix of excitement, trepidation, anxiety, and exhilaration, but once settled into the pilgrim's routine, the joy of the walk will surface.

*You've all been drawn to the path for different reasons. Each of you share a bond that will grow and spread into a grid. You will each experience the road as you have seen life show up for you, so let your mind open beyond the old ways of doing things. Survival, stress and all worries can be set aside, for when you are ready to go back to 'real' life the old ways may not be there anymore. Make space in your imagination that this is possible for you and that's what you will focus on and then notice as the days just flow. You will feel the ley lines as you approach the first city. Our own team of light assists you. This pilgrimage is meant to open the heart, open higher chakras, and bring about understanding of many of your past lives. Fear not, all shall arise for you. No one misses out on growth. All growth however is in your own timing. Keep in mind you are together for a reason and there are many reasons! ~ **Saint James***

*This trip is a lesson, so be prepared to love it or hate it, embrace it and grow in it. It's a mind trap to involve yourself in worry about the way you'll get up the trail. It is a path, and all must show up for it each day. ~ **Holy Mother Mary, Universal Angel***

*Peace upon you, dear ones. The path has been traveled successfully by seekers with the same questions since there has been a path. Should you go now? Why not? Remember, illusions serve to block the way. What illusions do you serve? Chocolate or vanilla, these details matter not. ~ **Saint Francis***

I was led to channel notes for our first meeting together at our breakfast group. I prepared the night before. This became my process.

*I see your heart of love, child, and ever watchful eye. Do not forget this path is yours as well. You are a signal, a light, but your light is valid to burnish. Encourage a dialogue with the group at dinner and ask that all share their triumphs and difficulties and their openings today. There will be issues to polish into shining gold and many changes to open the heart. Growth is held within the heart. No getting around it. Laugh, soul! It is life. Did you think it would be pain-free? Life, ah life! ~ **Santa Lucia to Me, Leon, The Pantheon Of Kings***

I met several Spanish saints that were new to me. Luckily our guide, Edi Picon was there to translate anytime I was stuck. I would describe the saint to the best of my abilities. Edi always knew their identity and told us stories.

23 September 2022, My Notes, Leon

Today we followed a guide through a church on a tour. We saw gigantic books in a room where I had a vision of a man in a red robe. When we turned to leave, I saw a painting of him on the wall. He was Saint Augustine. We all could feel the energy of the deceased beneath the church. We are in awe of the art and the architecture. Barb Manion bought me a notebook at the gift shop. Loose pieces of paper are just not going to cut it. There is too much to remember.

As a group, we are lollygaggers; loud, extremely happy Americans. We were excited to be sitting in outdoor cafés having a drink of summer wine and lemon soda with beer. There were children everywhere; their parents were having a beer and some tapas. Everyone was friendly and had a smile for us.

Edi reminded us of the difference between a tourist and a pilgrim. A tourist demands but a pilgrim is patient and humbly waits. We tried our best, but our exuberance couldn't be held in! We wanted to know everything! We were lucky to have the ultimate guide.

She has guided people on the Camino for 28 years and helped each of us in the group fall in love with Spain.

At The Santa Maria LaBlanca Church, O'cebreiro
Where the Miracle of the Camino Occurred

I cried my heart out and released a life of pain that I took on for the world (yes, it happens, and we forget), as well as several other lives when I lived in Spain.

I knew and deeply felt that I had a life nearby and in this church as a priest. The church felt like home to me and I felt the overwhelming pain and grief from that lifetime. Through my skills as a clairsentient, I received insight that goes further than just my intuition that I had lived there before. I was able to read the building and recognize my life was lived within it. My guardian angel, Holy Mary, reminded me to walk with others today. I must lift my spirits.

The group is functioning like a family now. There is always a handout, to make sure each one of us is okay. The human guides in our group keep a close eye on us as they know we are tired and feeling our emotions strongly. Our guide reminds us of the power of words. One of the best things you can do is get in the habit of speaking kindly to yourself and those around you.

Leon, Spain

*Children of the light, Sun, sound, and nature. Listen to your words, for they become stasis. They stick you right where you are and this is a lesson to practice on the path. With time and motivation, you will hear your words change into a language that can heal you, for are you not your own healer? Gently remind yourself of this again. ~ **Archangel Gabriel***

During our time in Spain, we had to trust that the language barrier could be managed. We soon learned that a smile, hand gestures, and kindness go along with patience. Soon, I learned important words like *bano, bolsa* and *mantequilla*! We were open to new foods and loved everything that was put before us! All fresh with nothing added!

At the first breakfast meeting our guides began the teaching by introducing themselves and setting the tone for what is to come each day.

Greetings! Each of us shall introduce ourselves.
　　I am Saint Francis, here in love and support of your beautiful hearts.
　　I am Mary, the mother of Christ, here as mother to each of you on your quest
　　I am Jesus, I shall help you remember to seek peace along the way. No matter what arises.
　　*I am Ascended Master Merlin here to help to open the heart! No worries, you all know me! There is the magic of the Violet Flame all around, you shall feel at home! Just so, dear seekers, for you are not ever forsaken. This path proves the point. Lifetimes of built-up pain shall dissipate. ~ **The Team of Light of the Camino de Santiago***

*Ask yourselves, is it better to be right or to be free? To walk a perfect Camino or seek the lessons upon the path? To love with judgment or with freedom? ~ **Archangel Michael, Astorga, Spain***

*Today starts an adventure. All of you together bring the energy of a group of pilgrims. Rest when you can. Listen to your guides, because one must be aware of a dynamic that begins right now. This group contains souls of six. But you will function energetically as one body, the each and the All. As a pilgrim, you seek the path. Remember to stay heart based as this time demands it. ~ **Saint Francis of Assisi***

*Do not worry about words, places, memory, body or mind. Your spirit carries you. Rest as the days flow into completion of your task at hand. ~ **Archangel Michael***

*I speak to you today as a Spanish traveler myself. Welcome, most glad you cleared the hurdles we placed for you! Of course, we did, you must mean it! For you leave Spain as another self. Take time in solitude on the walk for you shall begin to trust yourself. Remember, you always will honor each other. ~ **The Monk, Aymeric Picaud 1140 AD, French Monk, Barbadelo, Church of Santiago and Graveyard***

27 September 2022, My Notes, Portomarin

As we left Sarria, the start of the Last 100 kilometers, I met a woman who was walking the Camino with her family in celebration of her 85th birthday. She had recently lost her husband of 60+ years and was in both emotional and physical pain. I asked her permission to help heal her when my guides told me to offer assistance to her. This was the only help she would accept, as she rejected an offer to ride in our vehicle.

Ascended Master Jesus Christ taught me to spiritually feed when exhausted, hungry, or mentally in need of a boost. We used this in meditation each day. It is a matter of requesting it and the viscous liquid flows. He taught me the Shekinah Glory, a hands-on healing technique, before I left on the trip. I used this type of healing today. Her body was willing to continue, but her heart was heavy with the loss of her husband. I was able to assist and, of course, the others in the group offered their love and healing.

All types of pain were left behind on the path, and sometimes, we each walked separately in silence. Sometimes, we told stories and cried.

We spent the night at a beautiful ranch. It was the first time that I saw quince fruit growing on trees (it was evident that there had been a drought that year).

We saw Starlink overhead as we sat outside in the field and watched for ships in the night sky. I roomed together with Melanie. I hoped our laughter didn't wake up the others. We reviewed the photos she has taken each day. There are faces, letters, numbers, and information we need in them.

28 September 2022, the Manor House, My Notes, Touro

We met the Meigas in the grove. We stood in their circle and felt great energy lifting us. I was offered a gift of a bark heart from a tree. I declined, it felt like too much, too big a gift. It was such an ancient and comfortable feeling to channel a message in the essence of a language I'd never spoken in this current lifetime.

I knew I had been there before. The twisted trees surrounding us danced in the breeze like humans. There were very definite areas we could walk and explore, and some we were not to go near.

29 September 2022, My Notes

At the manor house I saw, in a vision, the Romans and the Spaniards fighting in the fields. Walking through the approach, out to the sacred forest at night, we saw so many orbs. The next day I walked through the gardens and felt the presence of the current owner's deceased mother. She lived in the house that had been owned by the same family for 300 years. It was so peaceful here. We cleared the energy of battle from the field.

The Team of Light gives us our food for thought each morning. Meditation first before even coffee!

This too, is my path to support. So take in deeply how far you have come and honor your journey. You are not the same. All heart's desires are needed to bubble up. Ask each to create this, as the mind imagines, so shall it flow. ~ **Holy Mother Mary, Universal Angel**

A humble request this morning to state these words: "An action is… A passion is… A focus is…" Ask and we can fulfill your dreams. ~ **Saint Francis, Morning Direction**

Always music inspires and clears on another level. Use this modality and all can see a huge release. Never discount the use of music to bring tears and unity. We hold you all in esteem, all working so hard together to become free! You have been shown precisely what is needed to ensure that all of you will never forget to notice what is around you ever again. You are little children at your first classes knowing the joy of learning! ~ **Saint Francis**

In this beautiful country, with such support, the hard knots of pain begin to unwind. Anger and frustration come up. Grief must be seen for what it is. The path pulls it out of us to be looked at.

31 September 2022

*Channel, last night was part of the true journey that coincided with the Small Group. All shall receive what they came for whether they know it now at this moment or not. Much more understanding comes as synchronicities upon the return home. When looking back at the easy illuminations, they shine bright, but the difficult and long-held pains that were released hold the best glow. Daughters and sons of the Way, I honor you for attending to us, as you are now ready to tell your story. ~ **Saint James***

Breath Work in The Castle by Amaral Valle-Torres

We were all invited by Amaral to sit in a breathwork class in a large room of the manor house. We brought pillows and something to lie down on. Some of us chose to sit in chairs. We were instructed by Amaral to breathe in and out through our mouth for 30 minutes. He showed us the pattern of breath, and then led us through it. At the end, he told us to grab our pillow and scream into it.

I'd never done breathwork before. The prana, or universal energy, builds and builds up and at the end the release, is exquisite. I had a vision that lasted most of the 30 minutes. People from my life came before me, living and deceased. I used this time to speak the *Ho'oponopono*, the Hawaiian forgiveness prayer.

I saw people from my life currently, and those I'd lost from the other side. I saw Queen Elizabeth, who had just passed away. I saw many people that made no sense as to why they were there. No matter, I prayed for them and searched for what was there to learn about myself. I saw a rolling golden light over Earth.

I felt like a limp dish towel at the end. Since then, I have done breathwork with Amaral as he teaches the class regularly over Zoom. I appreciate the peace the modality brings. You can move a lot of old energy out in a short time!

His information is listed at the end of this book.

The *Ho'oponopono* as I Say It:

I love you
I thank you
I'm sorry
I forgive you
Please forgive me, as I forgive myself

Mother Gaia steps forward during breathwork. I see Queen Elizabeth and quite a few of her family. I see over 100 people before the 30 minutes is up. Some are my friends and family.

Good day and welcome!
*   My own job is to hold close those who recognize me as home because life is constantly changing. Those who grow up on Earth can do themselves a favor to lean into constant change. There's much to learn every moment.*

Allow those of us who watch over you to help make your path easier.

What has been on your mind speaks to what has been in your heart. Great abundance shall always be present for those who reach out to that vibration and kindness with an open heart and understanding of flow. When you sense a moment of looking beyond yourself for this, simply give to another and flow resumes.

You are sensing other people's fear, lack, worry and anger; at not knowing precisely what is wrong Can you settle? As you settle, you project the frequency of rest and peace. There is a great need now for a feeling of peace to flow.

You are sensing a dying timeline. Many timelines are being seen simultaneously. That is why the channeling of a great grid holder was simply one aspect of soul. You saw the ripples of the aspects play across that individual's face. It is like a movie of many faces. As their total merging occurs, the connection will sound a different way.

Of course, a huge change has been felt the world over with the release of this grid. It couldn't help having a cataclysmic effect for that size grid holder to release.

*Depending on the work of the channel, an aspect of a soul will come through. One cannot see what one is not able or meant to see. ~ **Mother Gaia on the Death of Queen Elizabeth***

30 September 2022, Nearing Santiago de Compostela, My Notes:

Sitting for a rest, I have a vision. I can see a golden river flowing before me and I understand that is our goal for the day. We work together to flow this river ahead of us, clearing what has been left behind on this path. This is where people have come to lay down their burdens. Barb chose to sit with me. She is one of our strongest hikers. Sitting here, I feel held. The leg is holding up. I am so happy!

Our Teachers at Breakfast:

*Today is also a day for viewing old patterns. There are a few in this group who will lay down their long-held ways of how they have handled stress, grief, loss and daily life. Really, can life be better back home? You now have an example to strive for. ~ **The Monk Aymeric Picaud***

*On today's brief journey, you shall clear the residual from yesterday's issues that were pointed out. Resistance drains from each family member in this group. Trust over asking. ~ **Ascended Master Jesus Christ***

*Dust is as important as gold. No one is more important as each is right now. ~ **Lord Shiva to The Group***

*Are you honor bound? Are you living your truth every day? What is black and white and what is gray? What is the middle road for you? Your thoughts are now able to still while you walk upon the path. This is true freedom. But if your thoughts and emotions run your day, and your very life, you miss the peace and freedom. What is the action? Wake up from the dream that you are alone. Are there times in your life when your journey is singular? Those are the learning times and still you are never alone. ~ **Saint Francis***

*Child, listen to the humble bell on an animal. What is the thought of the sheep or the cow? It is the need for food, water and rest. Those will be your thoughts as a pilgrim. The animal is in tune with nature. The bell on her neck is no longer heard after its placement. The bell becomes the background sound of the day. The animal part of you, structures the day; with the rising and setting of the sun. Thus, the pain and discomfort each day upon arising shall fade into the background as you walk. Listen, souls, to your body's needs. Thoughts are present, yet they fade. ~ **Ascended Master Jesus Christ**

My Notes

The other members of the group have kept an eye on me. They know I am releasing my burdens on the way, just as they are. Amaral helps translate when the other guides are busy. He helped us cross water with a quick hand out.

Debbie O'Connor and I sang in the van today. The Bee Gees, "Stayin Alive." We cried for the times that to stay alive was all we could hope to do. We both sat in a little café and unfriended a few people who are no longer in our lives, and also some groups that are no longer relevant to us! Such a small act, but it feels so good knowing what is not important and not of my vibration any longer; time to let it all go.

Lavacolla, Spain

Today I met Mary Magdalene in the area where women would come together to wash before walking into Santiago de Compostela. She assured me we knew one another and since then she has become a regular guide.

At the village, I met myself. I knew without a doubt I'd been there, at that church, in another life. I vowed to come back and find my name in that lifetime.

Melanie's photos tell the story as light anomalies show up everywhere! Orbs and the blue light of Holy Mother Mary were seen in Amaral's photo at the church.

*"I am here as you walk closer to Santiago de Compostela. I will be with you. This route will be for grieving losses and as you know this must be done. Ungrieved pain and loss becomes pressure and pain held in the body." ~ **Saint James***

Reaching Santiago de Compostela, My Notes

What a great relief, we made it!

There is nothing like the feeling of walking into the Square and celebrating! There are so many people from all over the world!

The cathedral was overwhelming. There was a long line. The young man in front of me went in on his knees. A lovely older gentleman was ushered into the cathedral in front of us. He had the kindest eyes that reminded me of my dad. Later on, I noticed he was a priest sitting knee to knee with a pilgrim, giving guidance.

The energy there is indescribable. There are angels up near the ceilings that are many times bigger than a human. The energy of the relic of Saint James touched me deeply as he is a new guide of mine. I sat in a pew and prayed and gave thanks.

We had our Compostela signed. I cried, and the attendant came around the desk and hugged me. I believe this probably happens often. I was overwhelmed with it all. All the dominoes that had to fall to bring us together so far from home.

Fisterra, Spain, 25 September 2022, the End of the World, My Notes

There was a true miracle today! I'm glad Debbie was there with me when it happened. We broke off from the group to walk around to the other side of the lighthouse. We looked down into the rocks and suddenly I had a vision. I had been told by my friend and a powerful spiritual teacher, Pat Brack, that I would find a rock that would disintegrate in my hand and there I would see a vision. It unfolded exactly as she told me it would.

I saw Ascended Master Jesus Christ in front of me, but he was very, very tall. As I heard his words, I knew we had done what we came to do in Spain. Debbie felt the energy; we were truly in a different dimension together. When we came out of the vision, everything looked different. There's no way to get lost in this area. There's nowhere to go! It is a big oval loop. Somehow nothing looked the same to us and we had problems finding the van! After a while, we saw our group again and we were back to at least one dimension! Later in the van going back to Santiago, many of us were loudly singing. It occurred to me that most of us were not in our bodies. We grounded, and suddenly the whole van of people became silent and introspective.

I had forgotten about what Pat had told me in her vision of the disintegrating rock until it happened. It was a wonderful experience and such corroboration. Pat said, "You are not going to come home as the same person who went to Spain." I absolutely did not. I am brand new!

My Notes, Madrid, Spain

Some people went home after a few days spent in Santiago de Compostela. A few of us went on to Madrid. It has a completely different feel, and we had a great view from our hotel of busy streets in the downtown area.

The hotel is beautiful. There are many souls of the deceased in here and we soon began to understand that they wanted to speak to us. We assisted the souls that were ready to cross to the other side, but we had to draw boundaries in order to get a good night's sleep.

Several of us went to the Prado Museum. The energy that hit me as I stepped into the building was heavy. As usual, I became a bit disoriented with all of the energies. Also, just being in the presence of history and art is an overwhelming experience in 3D but if you add in the voices of the deceased and those who really want to get a message across along with seeing paintings I'd only read about, it was a little overwhelming.

Viewing the old master's paintings and sculptures will be something I will never forget.

It was time to go home. No need for lessons on the reverse trip, we were paying close attention. Our guides spoke about what may show up back at home after a life changing trip.

The crossroads show up when a person is ready to make their decision. The only way is forward. ~ **Holy Mother Mary, Universal Angel**

My dear one, the path to freedom! There had to be the fall after the loss. This, too, is a test. ~ **Saint Teresa**

The only test now is with yourself. ~ **Saint Eulalia**

What we missed when we came home:

The voice of the guides who spoke to us along the path.

The morning's lesson.

The daily walk in nature.

The simple food, the clear and pure, pure water we drank everywhere we went. Even right out of a communal tap! We missed the spiritual feeding.

The art and the architecture. The beauty of the land and its people.

The learning each day, the inspiration to do so.

The family feeling of love and camaraderie. The people we met during the day walking the Camino from all over the world.

The music that healed us.

The path with its symbols.

The body and its behavior under stress. The relief at the end of the day.

The knowledge that we were in the right place at the right time with the right support.

Re-entry from the Camino is not easy. I had no idea that many people would feel this way, but our group definitely missed each other. A year later we met up in a Zoom group twice and talked about the ways in which we have changed.

Edi, Our Tour Guide:

I think the most important question I have asked pilgrims at our final dinner together is "What have you learned? How have you CHANGED?" The change is inevitable even if you don't recognize it right away. However, the learning is constant with every step, every day. The re-entry is difficult because you've lost the everyday companionship of the group which has shared so many experiences. Experiences that would make no sense to anyone that has not walked the Camino. The physical pain is gone, your feet have healed and you've unpacked not only your bags but your soul. Sometimes that burden on your heart, mind and soul is heavier than we know."

The beauty of Spain is undeniable. The open and welcoming faces and great love of the area was communicated every day in the people we passed by on our journey. I dream about going back, and I know I will. There is always more to know about myself.

Tacoma, Washington, Summer, 2023

My Team speaks about the energy work The Small Group did together.

My dear, I come to you today as an emissary. We are ready to cut ties to old business that was connected to the tribes and now beyond. The business was dirty. We did not think it through. These cords you see are sticky. Will the small group hold the energy of each release and reclamation?

Thus, an ax bites through wood. Sometimes the blade meets rotted wood inside. The swing falls swiftly, but the powerful force was not needed as the rotten wood is easily severed. So this action shall go, as much rot falls into power without force. The time has arrived to cut out corruption. It starts with the original energy of the sins committed. So many generations have been blind to the original waste. Death occurs and the grieving must commence for the grief cleanses the wounds made by nothing but grief.

Come together as we connect. **~ General George Washington, 2023**

The Small Group connects with Washington, President Lincoln, President Jefferson, and Napoleon Bonaparte.

As you can imagine, this work has been done by several groups. Silent as the Small Group goes, those who blather do not interest us. No commotion needed only simple, hard work. Remind the group, you go as one. All directions needed to clear. It is a footprint you are after tonight. **~ General George Washington, 2023**

The river flows. The branches, sticks, twigs and debris have loosened, and the cooling waters have done their jobs. The wheel has turned. Observe the feeling of a new season. Time flies again if you've done your job of resting. Did you begin to take stock of what you will harvest this year? Allow yourself to believe in your own Abundance. **~ Princess Diana, Goddess of The Hunt**

15 September 2022

I am here to get you to see the black dragon. I am reunited now. I am a guardian angel to many. Some tell tall tales about me, but I am present in Heaven as an ambassador. Many simply could not see until the veil fell. **~ Diana as Princess**

San Xavier del Bac Mission, Tucson, Arizona, 3 February 2023

Moving To Pennsylvania

My Notes:

Missy and I have arrived in Tucson for the Rock and Gem Show. Warm weather in wintertime and the craziest streets I've ever seen! It's U-Turn city! The saguaro cactuses have captivated me.

I am overwhelmed at the rock show as soon as we get there. Rocks, taller and wider than me and giant rocks to sit on, rocks for sale on street corners and being sold from hotel rooms. It is such magnificent abundance! The energy is intense.

The Small Group told me that there is a place we must bring light to in Tucson. My friend also got the same message and sent me the photo of the church, just by chance. In the morning, I drove myself to a beautiful church on native land. Missy and the group supported from a distance as I was told to go there alone. Today's experience on the hill has me reeling. I sang down into the valley from the top of a small mountain as I watched so many souls cross over.

I believed that I would travel to Spain again in the fall of 2023. But then in March of that year, my guides began to nudge me with information that my husband and I might be moving. Sign after sign came to me, and we couldn't deny that we were ready to move on. So, instead of going to Spain, we traveled across the top of the United States to our brand-new home in Pennsylvania! Yes, a surprise. Pennsylvania is a beautiful state, and I am overjoyed to live here now.

The trip was a long one. We drove across ten states in eight days with four dogs in the backseat. They were excellent travelers. We made it just fine. The trip reminded me that grounding is number one. I grounded and cleared for the little family many times a day. We stayed wherever we could find a place that allowed four dogs. A couple hotels were really amazing places, and one place was rated only by the stars overhead!

I saw chain lightning for the first time over a valley in South Dakota at 2:00 a.m., along with my dog, Astro while on a potty run. We heard about an intense hailstorm later on that morning when a man at the gas station showed me his SUV dotted with dents. He laughed about it; he must've had the same feeling I did when I witnessed the chain lightning. I shook for quite a while when I finally got back to bed. It was exhilarating!

I gave my gratitude each day with my voice and drum at various stops with the Chiefs.

A highlight was a short trip to Bear Lodge or Devils Tower, in Wyoming. I was able to take some beautiful pictures, and I had a moment alone on the path where I was able to sing and say thank you.

We were able to stop to see the 50-foot stainless steel statue of Dignity of Earth and Sky, near Chamberlain, South Dakota. She looks over the Missouri river. What an amazing sight that was and I imagine even more impactful at night.

I was proud to put my feet in the heart of Turtle Island in South Dakota. I was told by Lauri to feel the heartbeat of the Mother, and I did!

My Guide, Stealthy Deer, Medicine Man, Puyallup, Washington State told me that I was led to the Conestoga River, which is near my new home. I have had many lifetimes here. He tells me I am safe by this waterway.

After we found our house and our offer was accepted, I went down to the banks of the Conestoga and played my drum to give my thanks. Below, Nikola Tesla speaks of great change.

All now are in form for the walk into the New Earth. The gate is open and those who are in timing for it and have made the statements and have had it written into their chart, have now walked into New Earth and it is done.

This has not happened yet worldwide because many are still not in that timing. The opening of New Earth has commenced as all of you have seen. Now it is time for the next step. There will be people *who need a bigger push to change, and they will get that push. They will get what they wrote into their own life's chart. If someone needs war, if someone needs the lesson to lose it all, if someone needs a health issue or a catastrophe, those things will happen. You can understand that all of you have gone through these types of things. There has been a war in the heart and mind of all of you. Now, most understand that peace is within you as well. It is a commitment to the process, to an understanding of the peaceful walk. ~ **Nikola Tesla, 17 March 2023***

*Greetings, the four of you represent directions. You couldn't be more different if you tried. Each of you sees things differently and what you've seen has been known in your past and past lives. Each way of seeing is completely valid. It is simply energy. It is an old belief system, and it is a new vision, all at the same time. You must ask yourself what is holding you in peace. And then let anything that is not holding you in peace go for it is time to rest. ~ **Mahatma Gandhi***

Allow me to fight for you. Yes, warriors are needed. You are all warriors of peace. That is the final word. The warrior symbol has been seen by many. It is the next step on the path. It is not the only next step on the path. Choose wisely. We support you in all moments.

*The Stone and Stars are full of assistance for all of you. What you will be doing walking forward will be seeking peaceful expressions for those who have not been able to see their way to New Earth and the peaceful path. I can't say it will be any different than that. You'll be holding those in trouble because there will be changes. And you know that some cannot see this yet. So yes, you've all had your experiences. Stay in the middle of the road. There's no reason to do anything else but the work in front of you today, that is all. ~ **Archangel Michael of The Sun***

*There is no need to wonder or worry about any of this as Nature is at the helm. ~ **Nikola Tesla***

"Patience, practice, surrender, and trust" were the watch words for 2023. My guides gave me the words "decide, partner, middle road, and listen" as the words for 2024. No matter where I am led to travel, or even to live, I am grateful for my many lessons over the last few years about remembering to listen and be watchful, because Spirit always shows up.

Chapter 10
Our Guides, Ourselves

To see in a higher and wider way through remembering is a relief. The life review was something to witness, and you see the reasons why it finally all happened. It is so beautiful in its simplicity. On Earth much is made over details. I had a lot of details going on! I was such an over-thinker and I worried, how I worried!

Worry eats away at joy. Go speak with your future self and believe what you see and hear. The future is fantastic! ~ ***A Beloved Friend Speaking from the Other Side after Transitioning, April 2023***

Just Who Are Our Guides?

No doubt some of our guides are aspects of us. I am a higher self and universal channel. Every day I call in the Creator, my higher self and my future self. Creator is always with us, but by calling in grounding and alignment, I focus myself on what is around me and within me.

I prefer my life with my guides in it! But I call them forward; they rarely show up on their own anymore. This keeps my day peaceful. If I see or sense someone within my energy field or nearby, and I haven't called them in, I'll ask them kindly but firmly to explain themselves or leave. It is important to keep our energy field as clear as possible.

One of my main guides is Chief Sealth. On this day, he was teaching me about seeing people clearly and showing me that I had a willingness to help, and I stayed longer than I should have in several situations.

I had to accept that I must step back. People learn in their own timing. When we step back, things change. Why hold acceptance now? Because any control, any perfectionism or any resistance keeps us right where we are. Acceptance brings the body into a peaceful state.

Then, true change can happen.

You have been learning compassion over and over again and to observe where you are in the moment. Do not fall, you have received the lesson, integrate it now. The up and down is a flow that you can now see better and be present to, than you ever could before. It's critical that you remind yourself that after the heights come the troughs. It's time to rest in these valleys by grounding. You've learned that if you do not keep up with your regular practices then you miss them. After today, you'll see you are responding well. You are learning not to run. ~ **Chief Sealth, Duwamish and Suquamish, Washington State**

I come to you to ask that you bind together with love towards one another. Look around and recognize the leaders in your community, your family and your world.

Be sure you are not blindly following false shepherds. If you walk like a sheep, be sure your leaders are not wolves.

It is time to recognize the beauty of all souls. You have truly been all skin colors in so many lives. By feeling pain, sadness, sorrow and anger and letting it pass through you, you'll better understand those with differences. Do not hold onto the fear that has the Earth held in its grip. One by one, together, we will loosen fear's grip. This begins with you in your own home, in your community. ~ **Holy Mother Mary, Universal Angel**

The realms have aligned, true. But just as it is taking time for humans to understand the energies present, so it takes time for all realms to align within their realm. The issues you are wrangling with are so personal. This is why overlaying a template on a huge idea is so difficult, it just doesn't fit. People can't even agree on what to pray for. The basic prayer of someone asking for their guides to save them is ever popular, and that prayer, while heard, does not show a willingness for you to work together with us for growth. Precision in the asking and a desire and the will to actually walk forward is needed in each human. For example, one has a plan that they wish to grow, and they ask for assistance on the first step of the plan. Does the human then begin to move to bring the plan into effect? No? There you see the disconnect. We are able to work with your hand in our hand. But your hands must be ready. Open eyes, open hands and above all, an open heart. What transpires after the request is up to each one. ~ **The Telosians, 2022**

Once one has forgiven and learned the lesson, grace flows. Standing up for yourself takes vigilance. ~ **Nostradamus**

Cleave to me, I am your anchor. Remember that The Holy Ones are the dry land. When you sink, call us in. All try one way or the other to resist learning lessons on Earth but still those lessons come. One cannot staunch an ocean. My girl, hold on, I am there. All on Earth are headed towards relief. ~ **Ascended Master Jesus Christ**

A friend sent me some beautiful photographs of open portals in her yard. This was the message from her galactic guides. They explained to me that most of us have a family group that assists us.

We are here for the purpose of guarding and communication. We assist when the light of the sun commences. As the light prior to this moment has come into the vessel, it has needed balance, tuning and movement both inside and around her human vessel. We are the contact. She senses us but fears a bit. We are not from this galaxy. This one requires our specific frequency. Channel may sense us now.

Sensing into these beings, I felt a high, light tingling, and pressure. I saw a tall Being come in very close. The Being told me that the movement coming in right now is assisting her balance. She required the balance codes.

We have come through Orion and are from far beyond it. As we help this one, she feels the movement. The movement assists her to balance. She has the belief that she is not well.

Further understanding regarding a beam of light near and over our homes came through a Lyran being:

This beam or portal of light is supportive to the human. We work together as a grid as well and you are ready to see a small part of our support now, take this energy if you wish as a higher key.

This key has been with you for lifetimes. Well done. You are free of that frequency (a clearing was done.) We will channel with you. There is more to know. The diamond is your new view of the support from all of us who have contracted to do this job. Think of us as coworkers. This friend was the catalyst for you to see our support.

We join with you from a higher quasar. Attend. Feel into it as if you are up, up and spinning. Feel through your feet and to your Earth Star chakra now.

Attend, for the water flows in alignment with many as we reach out to assist.

Record now, your photo helps people see us. Right now, there are examples that have been taken by people, but the ship is not seen by them. As personal frequencies rise, it shall become apparent that we are here. You have seen the light beams we hold over homes. If we are your family, we are here for you. You are attended personally by others as well. All information shall flow now.
*~ **Andromedans***

*The soul aligns, and I am with her. The field of possibilities is endless. We are and have always been. You are now able to experience the light into matter. The movement is a more dense experience. Before, your eye reacted after your energy field felt us nearby. Now the eye and brain are faster together. It is a new type of perception. There is no window now. ~ **Melanie's Angel***

*The ascension of Earth is our number one priority. We wish to bring a message through a voice of peace. Prosperity through peace is our number one goal. The glow, if you will, of the human is dimmed by 5G. We are here for balance. ~ **The Alpha Centauri from beyond the Firmament, a Mixed-Race Group including Pleiadians, Sirians, Lyrans, Arcturians and Avians Beings***

The resurrection of the human has been in full swing. While some have been focusing on the show, others have placed themselves in the river for cleansing and movement. Blinders were initially needed. Armor was de rigueur. Cutting oneself off was the only way, followed by enforced peace. But some are ready to come out of hibernation. The brain wakes up after some rehabilitation and care and the body follows right along.

Would you put sludgy fuel in your sports car? No, you paid good money for it. You lovingly restored it and you polished it up and fed it high octane fuel, didn't you? Same with your earthly vessel.

By now, with all the money you've spent on healthcare, you could have that race car! Your car is in the ditch or parked by the side of the road, you say? You know what to do. Drain and upgrade the engine and lovingly restore the body again with sleek bodywork. That chassis isn't obsolete yet. You have many more laps around the racetrack in you.

You've been that limping funny car. Get yourself up on the hoist and under diagnostics with us. An 18-point check and re-lube.

Here's a way to improve it. Water activated by the Sun, citrus fruit infusions, vitamin C and releasing the fear of 5G. Support your body with some adjustments, crystals, namely shungite, focused energetic upgrades or just plain loving care for the human body will make the biggest difference. By now your body knows how much it reacts to radiation.

Fear, medications, low vibrational food and the frequencies around the vessel add to this. All of you who have been weakened know about this by now. Many are just opening their eyes. Time will tell what will be added and deleted from your lives and only you can decide. The frequency of love overrides all. Even technology! Your body holds the greatest technology ever and you are finding out how to use it as a force for good.

We work with humans, animals, the angelic realm and the Inner Earth realm and more. Allow us to give you messages and we can find common ground.

Humanity is walking through a path made of fear known as The Dark. But it is truly made of overwhelming fear and staged to control which makes the human believe they are powerless. You are not.

In a group you are even more powerful. When more of you understand that this is happening, the Earth changes. We wish to support success for Earth. That is our goal. Earth and humans have been tricked and coerced for millennia.

We do not wish power over anyone. Our power is within and harnessed as peace, grounded peace.

That's where humanity shall prevail overall, when the majority chooses. It's never been done before. The ascension is divinely orchestrated in correct timing. ~ **Professor Albert Einstein**

Dearest ones, we are aware and ready. We hold the Earth grid along with the elementals and small Earth beings. No need to worry about the animals, what will be done shall be progress. Remember to care for your body. ~ **The Sasquatch, Elder Brothers and Sisters**

You witnessed an opening and took it. You are correct—it doesn't have to be graceful or pretty. As you have realized, change is messy. We welcome all into the deep green forest for transformation. ~ **Maeve The Meiga, Spain and Ireland**

I have chosen to have rest times where I do not contact my guides. Looking back on these times I understood that they were special to me as great soul growth occurred.

Guides are constantly stepping forward, and then stepping back again. Just like a big family, sometimes we don't see one another regularly. It is a celebration when we can be together again!

CHAPTER 11

The Chiefs, the Root Council and the Ancestors, Special Dates to Remember

Our thanks go to:

Chief East Lee, Lakota, Eagle Butte, South Dakota
Chief Sealth, Duwamish and Suquamish, Washington State
Chief Joseph, Nez Perce, Idaho
Chief Sitting Bull, Hunkpapa Lakota, South Dakota
Chief Red Cloud, Oglala Lakota, South Dakota
Chief Big Eagle, Mdewakanton Dakota, Minnesota
Chief Cornstalk, Shawnee, Pennsylvania
Chief Wilma Mankiller, Cherokee, Oklahoma
Chief Willenawah, Great Eagle of Tellico Corn Tassel, Cherokee, Oklahoma
Young Buffalo, Medicine Man, Apache, New Mexico
Grandfather Rainbow, Medicine Man, Puyallup and Tulalip, Washington State
Lorraine Joseph, Puyallup Tribe Elder, Shaker Church healer
    and spiritual warrior, Washington State
White Buffalo Calf Woman, Lakota, South Dakota
Bavado Blue Thunder, Shaman, Shoshone, Wyoming

Who is my guide? That is a question I hear often from clients. People want to know who is walking by their side day in and day out. We are the angel and the galactic, because after all, we live on planet Earth within the galaxy, and hail from far away. We have been part of nature; we have been fey.

When I answer the question about someone's guidance, I look around clairvoyantly to see who is around them. Then I look at what makes up their own human, body, mind, and spirit. Our soul is ongoing, but we have different experiences of the body we wear. We each have a guardian or guardians that have always been with us. Often that is one of the closest relationships we will have.

The Great Year of 2023

On 4 November 2023, the blue light came once again onto Earth strongly through the mesas in Arizona. The blue light is here to show us illusions and what we just could not see. There was a palpable change on Earth that continues.

Nancy Rebecca brought through this information years ago. She foretold the date and the places it would come in (N. Rebecca, 2023, personal communication). Please see Nancy's information in Metaphysicians and Groups.

I began to work with the Blue Light Column as part of the four directions in the Spring of 2023. Calling the blue light has been part of every circle since, every class and each time I meditate. This column grounds and rises us up.

We have noticed the Sun both changing color and increasing in strength. We are receiving a pouring-on from all of the suns through the great Central Sun.

The elementals work hand-in-hand with the Galactics during this ascension. The Golden Column of Light is held by the elementals as well as Archangel Metatron and Archangel Sandalphon holding space for the work.

In 2023 we began to know the freedom of No Mind. This may have felt a bit odd. The memory is not what it used to be and that is absolutely on target for this time.

We began to clear and return our family blood lines and by early 2024, we welcomed our ancestors back within us through the heart portal.

As we make statements about our life on New Earth, more and more opportunities arise as we speak our dreams out loud. The path is clear, and manifestation comes easily.

The breath we held over the last few years could be let go. What a relief!

The Monad merge on 22 October 2023 was felt around the world. This event raised the frequency of the entire planet according to Diana Cooper. The moment the blue light came in November 2023, heart chakras opened around the world according, to Nancy Rebecca (2023).

In 2023, I believed completely in the information I could both see and feel without pendulum confirmation. I still use my pendulum, but now I trust the information that I can see, feel, and hear even without it. Previously, I would seek confirmation through my guides as to what I could see in front of me in vision and pendulum confirmation. These days, information comes in blocks regularly. It's understandable through the higher senses. My guides call this central processing.

On 24 December 2023, I felt the sacred oil poured on my head. During the Christ hours of 24 to 27 December, all of us can feel this energy. I know this from inner guidance. This is an honor, a sacrament, that all may receive as an opening to assist in the rising up of ascension.

A dream changed the daily integration and reunification, a process that was part of my meditation for years, into the golden Christ Consciousness columns of blue and diamond light.

Gold has been a color I have been seeing for the past two years. There is a golden pathway and a golden platform that we use in the AOYE work for grounding and rising.

And as the Sun moved into Aquarius on 20 January 2024 and Pluto returned, the world felt the new epoch. Kali Yuga, a world age, is gone and done. Satya Yuga, the Golden Age brings in the New World.

January 2024, Morning Writing

At this moment
In this now
I release all that is ready to be released in peace and grace
I called in, as an open channel, my next step
And as I take that step, I believe I will then see another step
As I listen, I begin to see
When I see, I notice others
I gather together in witness and then opportunity shows itself
When I observe and add light, will I then, in turn, lift both myself and others?
This is my choice every day
This light can grow, but first I must observe it.

Did the body provide to you a commercial to watch and see how playing in the lower frequencies, perhaps with food, causes the body to speak up? Did it show you that eating lower energy food, and perhaps more of it, does not support you with all the resources you need?

Does your mind run a commercial about pushing yourself or doing something you really didn't want to do but had become a tradition during the holidays?

Being strong is no longer needed. The energy is not so heavy now. Change is easier.

In December 2023, you may have felt the frequency of being left behind.

We felt the return of the Sun on 21 December 2023 when all the great Suns aligned, and peace was felt from the Galactic core. Photonic light flowed in while Mercury, as the messenger, assisted with the ending of the Great Year, 2023. Grace manifests now and all will feel its silvery platinum essence.

On sharing the work of The Small Group

Chief Sealth tells me that the ceremonies are private, but the work of the Spirit is not.

Details are kept close for those that worked with the energy. What has happened upon Earth, we have participated in, but the details are kept between us for the privacy of certain individuals.

There has been talk of opening up and telling stories of what has occurred. Many groups have done this in their own timing from all parts of the world.

Much work on planet Earth was done through force. The work of this group, like others, has always been from love and peace. You have each listened well. We give you the right to tell stories now for it has always been our way to teach by doing so.

You have learned reverence for the land and the ancestors and the medicines. Some of you started only with long ago memories of these things. You kept your minds, hearts, and hands open and did the work.

As always, more work follows. This is the way. Come together and work it out. You have each broken down and rebuilt yourself. ~ **Chief Sitting Bull, Hunkpapa Lakota, South Dakota**

*We welcome this time together for stories and ideas. The days grow shorter. All of you feel the changes to Earth as her colors of green and straw liven up with the brilliant orange and earthy tones as the wheel turns. The sky and the planets show the movement and the changes as well. We see and file away the new to compare again the next day and night. Movement on all levels and layers are different now and the faster as well as the slower feeling readies the body for its next step. Very soon upon the planet will be the sights all cannot pass off as imagination. More fantastical stories, photos and amazement shall be revealed. Why wait to speak of it? ~ **Chief Sealth, Duwamish and Suquamish, Washington State, 24 October 2022***

The bright light of the future has much to teach us. We are no longer professional mourners. We have our own emotions and felt others' emotions and atrocities. Constantly prepared for resistance, in zero point, there is unconditional love and all pure potential. We stop thinking about healing and exist simply in the presence of health.

We are here to uncover the song of our soul that has always been.

The Small Group Witnesses a Celebration, Spring 2023, the Tribes Align and the Gates Open on New Earth

The Small Group gets psychic visions, dreams and nudges separately when we are to meet and work together. There will be messages in our daily photos and signs. We each knew something huge was about to happen. This combined vision was very emotional for us to witness. The Root Council speaks about this day:

Many gave their lives for their beliefs. This means freedom comes with a price and there is no growth without contraction. The Earth and its people are now living under the energy of growth.

Most felt nothing. That is just the way it is. For some, today is just another Tuesday. But by this time next week all will have noticed the change. The fear-lead people may read the changes as scary, but peaceful people will keep their eyes open and focus on their own business.

It is not a busy-ness time. It is slow-as-you-can-go time. Snow camp time. Keep warm, breathe.
*~ **Chief East Lee, Lakota, Eagle Butte, South Dakota***

*The celestial and terrestrial realms celebrate. This was the matter bringing cause to affect, the opening to the peaceful realms. A new frequency. What does it look like in the weeks to come? It depends on what you do, who you spend time with and their issues and your readiness to hold them while going through your own viewing. It could be chaotic or gentle. Decide now how you will react. Remember, it's a choice. ~ **Chief East Lee, Lakota, Eagle Butte, South Dakota***

*It is I who assists with time and timing with the Small Group. Celebrate with us today as this continues what we have longed for. Like an arrow's release, the muscles can relax now! Take your day slow and easy. Your body feels the lifetimes of tension. Your bodies are working when you are not working. ~ **Young Buffalo, Medicine Man, Apache, New Mexico***

*The power of a group of souls concerned with a particular soul, question or situation, shall increase the size or ability of the concern. We are with you now to increase your growth, the Small Group's growth and the quickness of its endeavors. ~ **The Council of Nine***

As the vision shows, you have died and returned. Died and returned. Do not deny your rest as you're learning to rest this lifetime. This goes for each of you.

If life is led from the heart, one counts blessings, even if the blessing is simply that you are alive today. For many that is their first thought in the morning. When the sun rises, your blessings are to be counted. This action makes them count! When a soul counts what is around them in their earthly trappings, the lesson is missed.

Those of you breathing the air this morning are blessed by the Creator. Those of you walking, even traveling in the mind are blessed to witness this transformation foreseen by generations. This sacred time upon Earth must be numbered as your greatest blessing on Earth or it will be missed.

*Do not be the soul that sits missing what is identified as the "good old days, the way it used to be". Label this moment as precious. This is your reality. If you do not, life will pass you by. What are your divine blessings today? In this valuing, this small action shall define your life. ~ **Chief Red Cloud, Oglala Lakota, South Dakota Speaking to Me one Early Morning***

*Just the fact that many are suffering and the request for true peace has been heard. The voices that are loudest are not always in the right. There is much screening of truth. You shall see more of what divides you, coming in the next days. All is not lost for anyone. Humanity shall rise again, even beyond what has occurred. We know you are hurting. Hold your peaceful stance and do not be alarmed. The kingdom of heaven awaits. ~ **Chief Sealth, Duwamish and Suquamish, Washington State, 11 October 2022.***

Mother Gaia supports us after the vision:

*The toning you are hearing in your left ear is adjusting your crystalline mental connection to planet earth. Ground, meditate and rest for we support you as your crystal grid supports you now. ~ **Mother Gaia***

Using the Art of Your Energy System with Pets

I went to Spirit2Spirit Ranch Equine Facilitated Healing Center in Stanwood, Washington in 2022 to meet two horses and teach them about the codes. I was a bit worried because I've always been afraid of horses. I haven't spent much time around them and I always felt like I didn't have a connection. My guides weighed in on this matter on the way up North to the ranch.

*Have patience with yourself! The communication shall happen, but you must listen closely. They will show you images. They know you are coming, we told them! This meeting is very important for your groups. It's time to learn that you can easily communicate with all animals. Do not rush. Be warm and love them. ~ **Chief Sealth, Duwamish and Suquamish, Washington State***

*Slow it goes! Proceed as usual. Trust and believe that the process will further unfold after your visit. Once you leave, they will speak amongst themselves. They are very intelligent and will read your intentions and heart easily. ~ **Nikola Tesla***

While in the barn with the two horses, I noticed a pair of goats that were extremely interested in what was going on inside. They kept peeking around the door to see what was up with the horses. I met the barn cats and other animals. During my visit to the ranch, I learned how wonderfully intuitive and how incredibly kind horses can be. By the end of my visit the horses were standing very close to me and 'mouthing' my coat. The owner of the ranch, Sonia Jorgensen, told me that these two horses don't normally act that way around strangers. We were able to trust one another. I left my fears behind in the presence of such huge healers!

Sonia later told me that the horse named Barney, felt so important after he was gifted the codes. She said his work took on new meaning for him. Barney is now doing his healing work on the other side. I am very grateful to have met him in the barn that day and again in spirit.

Lauri Wilson, master healer of many modalities, took the codes to another ranch to teach several horses how to use them to heal themselves. After being shown the sheet of the first 33 codes, a horse requested "the other ones" and was exactly right to ask for them! At that point, there were more codes and they kept on coming faster than I could write the books! That horse knew he needed a different code and wasn't shy to speak up!

Saying Goodbye to Our Beloved Pets

The death of a pet is grieved just as much as the death of any other beloved soul.

It can be a harder loss sometimes as a pet's love is an example of divine and unconditional love.

The space they take up in our lives is not easily or quickly closed. Take your time in your grieving when your beloved companion passes. We never forget them, and they often visit. Your other pets may grieve the loss of their friend and housemate. It takes time for all of us to come to terms with a pet's death and we must give ourselves the time we need.

In our house, we have pictures and the cremains of our dog, Chief, a fawn pug. He was raised with a black pug named Olive. We lost them both in the last few years. His little altar is on the mantle with crystals all around. There is a small copper bowl for a treat. Our Chihuahuas still miss their uncle Chief. Two of them were like little nephews to him. He raised them up and taught them all of his bad habits. Chief's real mom, Michelle and his other dad Ignacio join us in talking about both pugs quite a bit. This is our way to grieve.

Saint Francis Shows Me a Pet at the Crossroads, Deciding to Stay or to Go

The little soul rests. The family shall grieve the loss of a pet deeply. The pet soul goes on and always remembers their people whom they loved. Memory is a funny thing. The pull to the past can be painful or a balm to the soul, but it's always a connection back to those we love who are no longer on the Earth plane. The soul asks for a release from its owner.

A pet may return again to its family. Sometimes the pet has been with its family in a past life. They are our protectors, our familiars, our guides and our support. They often are buffers for stress and, sometimes, can take on illness for the family.

A Few Examples of Totem Animals I Have Seen Recently:

The beaver: truth
The porcupine: protection, strength
The capybara: adaptability and resourcefulness
The elephant: power, stability, family,
The Buffalo: strength, stability and abundance

Our totem animals may show up during readings. I often sense my own totem animals around me during ceremony or meditation. Even the most unusual animal can be a totem! I often see animals show up as messengers within a reading as well. Everybody knows the example of a red cardinal as a message from the other side. Here in Pennsylvania, my office window looks out into my yard where there are a lot of tall old trees. I see specific birds and little animals come through for people either in spirit or in body. It's even important to watch what the birds are doing when they come through with a message. Do you see a crow with a mouth full of food? Is it a woodpecker busily knocking on a tree? All of this can be meaningful. Also flocks of birds are often speaking as one, giving a message.

The Whales Speak

Whales and dragons have been active in people's imaginations and visions in this year of 2024. Both show up often in my classes as guides and messengers. Below, my Team of Light speaks of healing both physically and emotionally. Call in your whale and cetacean partners when you are near the water. Call in dragons anytime!

*We speak for the dragons that surround you. We are protectors and assist you with information gathering. During this moment of 04-04-2024, we partner with you. We meet with you when you are sleeping. Call upon us when you are awake and feel our joy! We bring with us the rainbow light for physical healing. ~ **The Blue Dragon of the Water and the Rainbow Dragons***

*We seek to emotionally balance the human. Whales, dolphins and porpoises work together to lift up the human. We teach and support. ~ **The whale collective***

On this day, I received two new Actions. It is a magical day of creation. I never know when I will receive a code, overlay, action, or any other teaching. It blooms in front of me, and I follow, writing and learning together with my guides. Below The Root Council reminds us to ground and to always stay heart minded. We fly and hear the subtle voices when we align with New Earth.

As roots grow underground, they also link between the trees. We support you in this way. The Root Council describes it: The roots drop from the heart. ~ **Chief East Lee, Lakota, Eagle Butte, South Dakota**

What we notice in another is ready to be worked on for ourselves.
    While the heart knows the mind still questions. ~ **Chief Sealth, Duwamish and Suquamish, Washington State**

CHAPTER 12

Decrees, Journeys and Abundance

A Decree is Written to Focus Us on an Issue at Hand. It is Best Said Out Loud.

I wrote this decree prior to finding my last two houses. The last time I added in specifics and received every last thing I asked for, except for a mantle! I pictured my house in my mind and saw us living there.

During our most recent move, I was a little bit more open about it. I didn't really know what houses looked like on the East Coast, never having spent much time there before. After driving around, I began to have opinions on where I would like to live and what type of house I would like to attract. I had a vision of a white kitchen and an entry into it from the garage. My little house was a surprise and fits all of our needs!

No surprise, there was the white kitchen and all the rest.

Moving Decree

I release all games I've played with Real Estate in all lifetimes

I release all timing issues around moving

I release over thinking around a new beginning or beginning again and creating a new life

I release all of my angst about finding a job, community, my soul family and new friends

I call in easily the best home for us that fits our physical needs and has

a neighborhood full of friendly people and lots of trees

The neighborhood has a peaceful feeling

You can add in any features that you and your family need to make it a home.

Numerology can help you find the correct city, address, etc. and was very valuable to us. Deborah Stelfox, The Love Guru, helped me with our numerology before we moved. Her information is in the Metaphysicians page.

Programs such as "I can't go forward, I'll always be stuck, I'll always be ill, and I can't recover" must be released. Health is the body's natural state. Releasing these thoughts in the mind with their continuous looping is entirely possible.

Health is my goal, so to support that, I choose:
A healthy diet
Exercise every day
Creative pursuits
Friends around me that I can reach out to when I need help
Regular daily spiritual practices

Holy Mother Mary, Universal Angel, Separation Decree

Mother Mary taught me this decree. Say out loud in humbleness, in love and with divine gratitude, I release (say the name) from all contracts we hold together:

I make null and void all old contracts from this lifetime, from past lifetimes, and all timelines.
Between us, I see the golden light of healing. The pearl and diamond light comes in and separates us easily.
I am thankful for this lesson that taught me that I have the power to use my voice and that my grounding is firm where I stand in my power and station.
And from this grounded power I say: "I release you. My contract is finished. Thank you for the lesson."

I imagine a bubble of pink light around me. It flows out from my heart. I say, "Thank you, Holy Mary, for your attention, protection and love. So, it is. It is finished."

When we realize difficult situations happen to everyone, even the most spiritual wizard still gets flat tires, still loses friends, and sometimes still loses a job.

We learned that it's how we react to keep the ball in play that shores up our energy and then, soon, life shows up again as easy, open, and possible.

Watch for that old jingle that goes through our head when the tire blows or we are overdrawn at the bank and our car doesn't work when we try to start it…

- I knew that would happen!

- I was waiting for the other shoe to drop!

- This always happens to me just when things are going so well

Mental Health Decree

I command to release any and all programs, known or unknown, around mental health
I train my thoughts to come from the heart and a higher level of focus and care
I keep a journal
I speak up when I have needs
I take time to lovingly care for myself
I keep track of my food and water
I rest when the body and mind are tired

It takes a few seconds for an emotion to run through you. If you are present, and in the body, you can feel it flow through you.

It might feel like tingling, zap, or a feeling of weight in your belly. If you are holding this emotion inside the mind, mental field, and old habits have started to keep it in your energy field by thinking about it, this emotional feeling will stick.

Old emotions build up and become sticky like tar. Over the years, this adds up as "weight" in the body. The feelings and emotions form a body of pain.

When ready, a pain body, as I see it, will show itself and we can release and clear it.

The mind is on where the details will be focused and gone over and over again and again. We believe we are "working it out" for "clarity" but, instead, let your beautiful imagination run wild! Imagine ways of releasing these stuck emotions. Just like a little movie, create symbols and see them and, most importantly, feel them rise up and out of your body.

Intention, Dialogue and Imagination

Call in the Creator. Call in your higher self and your future self. Ask for what you need. Allow, give yourself permission and come into your heart space to gently release what you have previously stopped from moving through you. Forgive yourself if you need to. You are not "at fault."

Imagine your heart opening up. Tap on your heart and speak out loud. Intend to release old looping thoughts and emotions.

> *"Body, today we will work together to release grief. We are ready to meditate, and during the meditation, we will be feeling and releasing old memories and stuck emotions."*

Imagine symbols and shapes rising out of you. Focus on your breath as you do this on each out-breath, imagine light, smoke, symbols, or confetti releasing out of you until your imagination takes over easily without prompting. This is your beautiful imagination at work! Along with your guidance team, work together with your imagination to make it easier.

The Child Within Decree

I love you, my child self
I honor you by giving myself permission to play and use our beautiful imagination to create!
We will put our hands in the dirt. Paint and draw. Color!
We will dream as we lie under the stars. Find the constellations and name
    them. We will lie down on the grass and watch the clouds float by.
We will make up songs and sing them loudly! We will laugh with our
    friends and get down on the floor and play with our pets.
You are a beautiful part of me and I honor you.
Thank you, my inner child. I love you.

Releasing Archons

Archons are old controllers, master manipulators that wind up and push those niggling worries and keep us stuck. They use our energy by attaching to us and sucking us dry. It is up to us to release them because they are ready to be released. It is time!

Archonic presences feel like a heavy weight in our body similar to entities and the dead. You may notice bloating and a pressurized feeling in the body. Or you may notice nothing if they have been there for a long time.

When I see them in the energy field of a client, together we acknowledge them and break the ties. It is a great relief to release them.

If you have looping patterns, call in Saint Joan of Arc, and ask her to help you release the Archonic presences within you.

All of these practices are easy to do when you remember that *clair* senses are human skills. You no doubt have noticed that clairvoyance, clairaudience, mediumship, and maybe even your empathy has changed and increased over the last couple of years.

To become proficient at these skills it takes time, patience and focus. Have fun during practice and, as each skill comes on line, celebrate the small and large gains! Give yourself permission and allow yourself to be creative and daydream. We were taught that daydreaming was a waste of time, but it is both a rest for the mind and a big part of growing your higher skills. These skills show up with color and movement. It can be subtle, then one day it is not subtle, it's brighter and easier! Become aware of the changes in your meditation. This is where you will see new colors and new symbols show up.

The opening of your skills may have happened as a child. You might have seen things and went into a fearful state. Perhaps you had no one to believe you. Or people said you were lying about what you saw. At this point some people completely slam the door shut. Then comes a time where you are ready to be yourself and accept these abilities. Supporting the physical body is imperative as you grow your skills.

Healing others or offering healing through the universal energy field does not cost your body energy or resources. Remember the true healer is the client—we just hold the space for the healing to occur, use our skills and shine a loving light.

Prior to any meditation or journey, we call in together:

> The Golden Columns of Light to hold our space, Star and Stone
> The Stargate, our octahedron and travel ship of information
> The Violet Flame of transmutation and clearing of lower energies
> The Blue Light Column to both ground and rise up

"Feel, see, sense, and imagine" is said at the start of every journey for each of us experiences the journey in our own way. In the AOYE practice, we call in sacred geometry around us as we walk onto the selenite path, the green grass, or the dirt—out to any platform that shows up in the journeys or meditations.

The 6D selenite path is a sacred space where changes occur. There is a golden grid upon this path. Try it!

A journey may sound like: *You are heading now to the selenite bowl. The selenite bowl is the symbol for zero point. There are three eights in the middle of the bottom of the selenite bowl. We place our feet there to bring us back into polarity. Once you are here in Zero Point, the clearing is called in.*

What's in a Picture?

You also may have noticed that you can "see" what is around you in a subtle but powerful way. You may be able to pick out light anomalies showing up in photos, symbols or faces.

Paraidolia is the term for seeing faces in photos, art or inanimate objects.

But what about faces in nature?

The human brain searches for patterns, but the clairvoyant sees symbols. When one is open and available to the "new" energy, there are visions of Inner Earth, Earth, and Star to be seen everywhere! As we grow in our skills and our own energy advances, it is easier to see what is around us and inside the human body.

Using the flow of Power Vs Force

No one has the right of power over another. Yes or no must be stated. When you are in your own power, the rest is noise. Then it is not even noise, it's just… nothing.

Coming into the understanding that we truly have no control and never have, or really needed it, is quite freeing. The only power we need is in the unified field of energy around us and our own human skills.

The Earth and its inhabitants have been in duality. As our frequency rises, we find ourselves in several dimensions at one time:

3D separation, materialism, duality.

4D, the Astral, beginning awareness of universal law, what affects one person affects everyone. Unity consciousness. This is where the work on ourselves begins.

5D no linear time, unconditional love and living from the heart.

Working on judgment, guilt and psychic development.

6D We are conscious of miracles, aware of dimensional realms.

And so it goes, above and beyond. Constantly, remembering that grounding must happen first.

Money and Further Abundance

Self-empowerment, self-esteem and self-confidence will grow with patience and dedication to changing your life for the better.

You don't need to know all of the why's and when's. These things get uncovered in timing, exactly when you are ready. Clarity doesn't show up every time we'd like it to but if you are willing to sit with your emotions and develop a grounding and clearing practice that you use every day, you will have your understanding, if you still need it. You might just feel better and forget what you thought you needed to know.

Healthy sexuality and a sense of freedom are possible at the same time. One begins to understand that there is physical power in the orgasm that clears the body in its own unique and healthy way. No wonder a female's sexuality has always been blocked by force. but women are taking their power back, as the essence of the divine feminine and divine masculine are becoming aligned world over. The time has arrived on Earth when men are more able to express their feelings of being overwhelmed, out of balance and having had to conform to society's image of the male.

Being unable to love our own bodies, just as they are, has been part of the programs offered to us by society. The focus on perfection ladled out by AI, advertising, magazines, and movie 'standards' has us believing we are not okay without the products they want to sell us.

Creator loves you in this body that you designed in precisely the way it appears to you now. Your higher self loves your body. Ask yourself who or what did you give your power away to?

Victim

Remember to return to you, any soul piece lost during a time of power struggle. Power is not force. Power is the embodiment of Source accessed through your heart. If sex has ever been an obligation, implied or taken from you without your consent, you may hold resentment and contempt resulting from that trauma.

You are no one's victim. Talk about what happened to you with those you trust. Get help so that you can heal.

Money

Money is always around you, it's an energetic level.

If you were ever just about to obtain money, and if you did not receive money that was available or was right in front of you, or if there ever was any type of energetic block between you or money, believe that the money is still there—because abundance is just a frequency!

When you align with the frequency of abundance, all types of abundance will flow. It is the same with love, jobs, friendships—no matter what happened to you that stopped these things, once the blockage to abundance is removed, this frequency will flood in.

What stops abundance? Looking at the situation through a telescope backwards is a symbol I see when a client is ready to align to a more abundant life. We must look at our deep feelings and family patterns about living in abundance. We then mine our sneaky subconscious about staying in a lack based pattern. Also, the lack may show up when we look at past lives.

When one cannot recognize abundance for what it is, we are out of balance. A trauma may have happened that prevented you from taking risks outside your comfort zone or even just being able to take a chance, knowing you hold the ability to fail and rise again. The mind might throw up all kinds of reasons not to take a job, go on a date or just about anything that scares or stops you.

First the blockage is cleared in every reading or class, and then the six abundance codes are sent. These codes are taught in the AOYE II class.

We must accept that the universe always tests us. If we are in balance and recognize a test for what it is, we can simply accept that test and move forward. This is the symbol of the middle road. A little red flag overlooked or set aside will bring a bigger flappier red flag, and then along comes a little lesson. And, if you didn't pay attention, then a bigger one will show up! This is why we clear and ground ourselves every day so that we can see those little signs! We drink water for the cleanse it provides but also so that our brain functions well. It is not enough anymore to sip a bit of water from a straw here and there! Become a regular water drinker, enough to support the size of your physical vessel. You will notice everything runs better, mind and body!

CHAPTER 13

The New Skills and The Overlays

The first Art of Your Energy codes came in, followed by the skills, and then came the overlays. Then more codes showed up in timing until now we have 111 of them. The Art Of Your Energy card deck has all 111 codes featured.

Next the actions came in. And so it goes as the modality develops.

I teach classes in the Art of Your Energy and the skills, The Ladder and Code Combining, are taught separately. This modality clears even the deepest old wounds. Holy Mother Mary, Universal Angel gifts us a beautiful way to let go of old pain and labels.

I am speaking to light up your bravery and continued attention to finding and releasing painful memories and stuck emotions from all blaming situations within the family that you grew up in or are living in right now.

*Can you remember some things you were blamed for in your nuclear family? Imagine some things such as being too much, too loud, too sensitive, angry, sad in grief, or too different. You were you. You were different. Give yourself a moment to imagine you have in your hand a small prayer flag and a pen. Write a few things on each flag. Allow the breeze to purify these labels you were given and are now able to release. Name them. Let them go! ~ **Holy Mother Mary, Universal Angel***

Lock and Key

The skill called, "Universal Lock and Key and Offset" is taught during The Art of Your Energy II. There are ten categories of possible situations, emotions, and feelings with names, such as Silence, Dynamite, and Underwater.

If the client is ready, Universal Lock and Key allows for an unlocking of trauma and a release of stuck emotions and feelings that have occurred within and around a traumatic event.

The skill called, "The Ladder" is both a code and a process. It is also a spiritual tool. The Ladder skill looks at where the client became stuck.

The Ladder is made up of a 15-part code/list, including the Warrior, Justice, and the Advanced Game.

In the code image, the ladder and the path are shown together. The ladder speaks to where you are, and the path shows where you advance. The ladder is also a viewing device for the clairvoyant to see the path and where you became stuck.

The ladder code itself is a multi-part code that clears and assists with breakthroughs, activates weight loss, and substance release. The ladder codes work with chakras and crystals.

Code Combinations is a set of 13 codes combined in a way that clears several issues at once. For example, #6 There Are No Others uses a code for struggle with others, together with a code that bursts us through the glass ceiling, if we are ready.

Code combinations are powerful actions. My Team of Light describes the moment when we are ready to act:

Within this modality, understand that the heart is the portal we work with. Zero point is the ignition, and the Violet Flame is the optimizer. ~ **Nostradamus, Speaking to the Class in June 2022**

All are ready for this moment of change, whether they realize it or not. It is not up to one to judge another's path and to point out the action, as the act of judging may bounce back on the person who views another in lack. There's actually no lack, as this world is complete with an abundant flow, as well as many walls and lessons to teach this truth.

Lessons on the path and a short road to nowhere are common parts of an individual's life. When these are observed with little emotion and no charge is present, one begins to see the hold thoughts and noise has over a life. We are not speaking about emotions as they are all beautifully perfect and in a range that a human can access for growth and comfort. The noise I speak up is a boundary to growth. ~ **Ascended Master Sananda, regarding family programs and patterns**

Let us begin by reminding all that your life is defined by you. If one agrees and works to define it as a full life; at the end of that life, one will look back to see what was created. The human is in the void space at this moment, true, but many are still in a prison of their own making. If you are already free, may you be an example to those still stuck in the mire. Just by your example you awaken the world, one person next to you, at a time. No need for force. Just your beautiful example of removing the corral or pen that held you fast.

A horse freed does not long for the corral once it has seen the pasture and what is beyond it. My wish for you is to trust there is a further world. This world is in front of you which can be accessed by releasing the hold of the mind. A busy mind focused on traveling the cosmos is a gentle mind indeed. ~ **Chief Sitting Bull, Hunkpapa Lakota, South Dakota, 2022**

The morning sunlight plays over Earth, lighting up the new world. Visions of Spring fills the mind with the possibilities of new growth on the trees and green lands. Know that your own tender new shoots of confident growth feel the wonder of change over the Earth and within you. There is no stopping it. Yes, hard rains come and gray clouds descend into the valley now, but does that moment stop the tree from its seasonal shifting? No, nor should it stop you. Part of your growth is the stages of comfort and discomfort from the hardship to the possibilities of change that push you, the release is sweet. Step aside for Nature's turn is upon you for inspiration and marvel.

*There is a cave I know. Once per day for the short while I stayed there, it was lit by strong light entirely. Other times the dark flooded in. The light within my soul sustained me. It is your choice now to hear a message and hear it clearly from the heart. If it is your message and the voice is loud and clear, take to the wind. Work together with your guides for there is more to learn. Child of peace, drop your sword. No more are you chased. The mind releases if you let it. All assistance is always through your own family as we are and always will be. ~ **Mary Magdalene***

*The resurrection of the human has been in full swing. While some have been focused on the show, others place themselves in the river for cleansing and movement. Blinders were initially needed. Armor was added and cutting oneself off was the only way, followed by a forced peace. But some are ready to come out of hibernation. The brain wakes up after some rehabilitation and care, and the body follows right along. Would you put sludgy fuel in your sports car? No, you paid good money for it! You lovingly restored it! You polished it up and fed it high octane fuel—same with your earthly vessel. By now, with all the money you've spent on self-healing care, the real kind, you could've had that race car. So your car is in the ditch or parked? You know what to do! Care for the engine and lovingly restore yourself again with good body work. You have many more laps around the racetrack in you yet. Get yourself up on the hoist and under diagnostics with us for an 18-point check and re-lube. ~ **Professor Albert Einstein on Working on Yourself, 7 April 2023***

Most of my guides have a great sense of humor. I love to laugh and appreciate them teaching in this manner. Some are gentle; some come through in great power and are matter of fact. As you get used to communicating with them, it is very easy to recognize their frequency and voices.

Multi-Dimensional Field and System Optimization

In my class called "Illness Goggles," we were reminded that once we tune our glasses to see ourselves better, we will perceive symptoms and issues change for the better. Just by changing your words and keeping a close eye on how you speak about yourself, you will remind yourself that you are YOU first and not a walking diabetic, autistic, or bipolar person or any other such label.

Once you begin to accept that you are you with your own type of symptoms, your focus changes to working on the symptoms one at a time.

Have you ever had to prove that you are ill? Are you one of many who have an autoimmune illness where it's very important to make sure you work on keeping yourself rested and as healthy as possible, but no one can see that you have many days that are difficult? If someone does not support you or doesn't believe that you do not feel well, make sure you understand that this judgement issue is on them and in their perception. Can you be happy and successful while living with an illness or disability? Of course you can. Untangling what you believe about your illness or condition, aside from what others believe, can set you free.

Remember that wherever you find yourself on your pathway, begin to focus on healing your story that brought you to the spot where you are stuck. Find within yourself the deepest respect for how far you've come and what has happened to get you here. Recognize the words you use and your style of talking about your body or symptoms.

Ask yourself if your living situation is a soft pillar to land on, a sanctuary or just part of the noise around you? Rest, quiet, and unplugging must be a part of your day, and that is non-negotiable. Your mental and emotional health must become a priority with regular relief of built-up pressure. Find a friend to talk to. Determine ahead of time who has the time and the mental space to listen. Make it a fun journey, a walk outside. It only costs you the decision to make time for your mental health.

Welcome the trigger—don't push it away. Recognize when you become anxious or upset when others around you are anxious and upset. Once triggered and emotional, the emotion belongs to you, and it's up to you to identify and work through it.

Make a plan.

The people around me that have successfully healed themselves have made their wellness a priority. They use some combination of Western and Eastern medicine, and energetic healing, with a focus on cleaner diet, exercise, and mental and emotional healing.

Finding the peace, the wonder, and the magic that it brings to your day is worth every trial you had to go through to choose yourself first, over and over again. By simply (and everyone looks back and says it was easier than they ever thought it could be!) unplugging from what used to hold you stuck, you are then free to take time for yourself without giving yourself a hard time about it. You are worth every moment spent in peace! The Buddha describes it as the middle road:

The truth is a wheel that spins with opinions and the knowledge of what is birthed brand new. The truth is the teachings of all life by simply weaving Nature and human nature.

The knowledge and song of the planets and stars and the path between your feet. Just consider all these things as you walk the middle road. ~ ***GauTama Siddhartha, The Buddha on Staying in Peace***

Excerpts from My Classes

From my class "Out of body? Come On Back In!"

This is an exercise to better understand those souls around with whom you have an agreement and with whom you have walked down the bumpy path together.

Arrive at the auditorium. Take your place on the stage. Look down at a room filled with people. Find the people who have hurt you looking back at you from the very first row.

The second row holds people who didn't assist you when they could have, they chose to be neutral, or they did not show up for you. The next few rows hold friends, family and coworkers who have had a spot in your life, but do not hold roles that you named "healing, helping and supporting". Take note as to who showed up and where they sat.

The back rows are full of people that, over the years, have been very instructive in life in one or two ways. They have helped you or they have taught you lessons that you marked "very good, helpful, and good but hard."

Say "hello" to another row or two of smiling beautiful people that you have lost one way or another. Some of these people may be deceased. Look at the faces of these folks who came for you today. Feel the emotions in your heart.

The last rows are jammed full of ancestors! Look at this diverse group. They send positive healing vibrations towards you. Pull that energy frequency in and feel it!

In the final row, see the beings of light: angels, galactic beings, and other realms and aspects of you. How does this feel?

Send the entire auditorium all the love you can muster directly from your beautiful heart. Your entire energy field glows with beautiful pink light. See roses began to rain down, bright, pink roses, pastel pink roses, and rose petals everywhere, covering the feet of all the people who came for you today.

Each soul in this place of highest healing has had a hand in your growth. Go back to thank each person row by row without labeling them. They are each another form of you!

In the class, It's All About You, Baby! We release in ease and grace

- All the times I have agreed when I didn't want to

- All the times I chose someone else's needs over mine

- All the times I gave in

- All the times I took less than what I was worth

- All the times I held on when letting go would have freed me

Drama Llama

People felt prompted to take the class called, "Drama Llama" either because they have noticed dramatic emotions around them or in someone close to them. They made the connection that it's time to take a look at releasing drama.

How does one become a Llama? This takes place when any size issue is unable to be easily processed and then grows in the mind and sticks into the mental or emotional body.

Growing up, you may have learned to express feelings from another llama. Llamas view their lives dramatically and often then speak their worries and anxiety into existence. Then the mind loops without making room for another more positive scenario, and then, depending on what we focus on, drives in situations for more confirmation that the Llama is correct

What to do if YOU are a recovering Llama?

- Watch your words, make sure they are neutral, 'sterling' or positive

- Watch your thoughts and trace them to the past

- Watch your triggers as they all have a red cord back to the beginning of when they were developed

- Stop wondering how others think or will react to you or a situation

- When the Llama-self shows up, ground and clear, sit with the emotions of what came up for you, without judgement

- Speak less and listen more

You got what you wanted, now what?

You may find that you slip into a time of quiet.

Be brave and hear yourself in this newly available way. The clarity you have sought all your life is arriving.

Trust yourself to notice this! It's a door illuminated by the Sun and available to all!

Do not doubt that this is within you to uncover, as our frequency rises and we work with manifestation, we begin to see the energy of all things. We begin to truly understand that what we hold within our minds can appear before us one way or another.

We are attractor beings of amazing abundance and, sometimes, we attract the same old thing. If this happens to you, there is now a choice to make. What happens if we receive what we've seen in a vision, but then, as we move through each stage of the path, our old patterns return? In this new energy of peaceful focus, we stop and release as soon as we sense a pattern, a trigger or old pain that has returned.

The Small World

Remember, everything and everyone in the realms will speak with us if we come in peace with an open heart.

Master Buddha calls the world of bugs and insects the "Small World." They are trying hard to get us to pay attention! It took many mosquito bites and photos of that realm within a realm to force my attention to understand that they wished to speak to me. In the summer of 2023, I worked with the Avians, and it wasn't a stretch to understand that the bugs and insects wanted to connect, too. It is a huge realm, and each species supports one another. We must recognize the fact that the human race does not do this as well as Nature does.

Ear toning is another example. If we get quiet, there are tones within tones that come into our understanding. The tones can be messages, but we cannot access this when the mind leads the way. When the heart leads the way, there are no questions about what to do. We begin to truly listen. As you begin to hear your higher self, your future self, higher and highest aspects, you will understand the softness and subtlety of that inner voice. That is you speaking.

17 September 2023 Eclipse Corridor

In my class called, "Walking the Earth's Grid," we came in contact with the stone realm. The Sha of the Stone Realm tell us that people often try to release and remove them unknowingly, but as part of Earth itself, they are up to the greatest good as they are meant to be players in the system of natural clearing. They show up as a large mass of positive energy. As a group, we match up our energetic codes with theirs and then observe the world underground where we live.

The Sha realm was identified to me years ago by a seer when they were ready to speak to me, but I only recently understood its connection to the word 'shaman', a Sanskrit word meaning healer or person who works with Nature and can communicate with it. Several cultures have words with the same root identifying those of us who hold the land sacred.

We picked a spot in our yard or a place where we go to meditate to begin the journey.

We were told to review the record keeper crystals of the Earth. These are the crystals that hold information of what has taken place where you live and walk. The energy and data of conflict, death, sadness, danger and also happy and light energies can be felt.

The particular energy when entering an especially violent field or even a sacred space can be sensed through the body as tingling, a heavy weight, coldness, or warmth. Though time passes, the Earth remembers. As healers, you are either adding to the health of Earth or enforcing what is already in place.

It is our daily choice, isn't it? How can we do it alone? Remember, we are never really alone! And we can be armed with belief and intention to clear what is under our feet, thereby offering a better energy to flow.

In class, we intended to feel the flow of the grid beneath our feet and took notice if we could feel it in both feet. We tuned into the Sha realm, a group assisting Earth. We felt around for a disconnected place or a thready energy or a pinch. We asked the realm to assist us in clearing the blocked places in front of us. If you are clairvoyant, you may see the stones under your feet align. Use all of your senses to assist and intend to clear your spine at the same time.

We were held by the Indigenous Chiefs, medicine men and women, and as always, the four directions. Long ago when our feet were bare all day and we were one together with the seasons, we planted crops by the Sun, found our way with starlight, knew within our deepest heart that we came from the Stars. We lived close to those we loved and revered the Ancestors.

We are still these people, they are us now, and it's easier than ever to claim our sacred blueprint as part of Earth and Sky.

The mycelium below our feet is a living world of communication.

Mycelium is a vital food source to invertebrates in the soil. It grows in water and even moves water around. It aids in soil decomposition and keeps plants and trees healthy.

Mycelium sends out information and warns of incoming danger, sometimes as a body that is acres wide.

When I asked if the mycelium wished to speak, this is what I heard:

We support and are a vital food source to many. We extend out to the deepest and furthest places seen and unseen. Our thread-like structures are often overlooked but our job is to be used. We serve. We thank you for noticing.

Trees are communicators, the ultimate observers!

If you are having a hard day, take even a few minutes to go outside near a tree or, better yet, touch a tree, as this energy can bring us back into flow. Trees remind us of how great it feels to place our roots into the ground!

A mighty oak five stories tall, a little apple sapling just starting out, a majestic redwood or a happy holly tree all feel completely different to the touch and other senses.

You have probably had a relationship with a tree! Remember your favorite climbing tree or the one you visit with daily on your walk? Think of the one you mourned when it was cut down. It is time to honor the trees as they are the stabilizers of planet Earth.

*Yes, we see you with the weight of your good days and hard times. We sing out our natural frequencies and hold you as you struggle. We would be happy to accept your gift of love today. Sometimes we are only thought about when we are in the way, making a mess or are needed for something you want. Please think of us as friends and collaborators. Earth is changing, you are, too. Our communication these days is louder, direct and easier heard. Join up with us as partners in healing. For as Earth heals, you heal and as you listen to your body and what is around it, your healing accelerates. ~ **The Tree Realm***

*I am the speaker for the trees tonight. Spend time with me as I am your guide. Get comfortable with all who speak from the trees. The four directions hold you as we dip into the realm of the trees and the mycelium's own grid. Sense around you the golden hour. Feel its light. We speak most in the morning and evenings in golden light. Feel us hold you now and sense or imagine a cocoon a foot above your head and now heading into the tops of the trees. Feel your body flow back as your feet rise. Relax. Come up and rest with us now. ~ **The Living Tree Speaks through The Great Golden Owl***

The Great Listening Place

Trees can teach us how to be better observers. Rise in meditation to the top of the Living Tree. Get comfortable in its never-ending branches. Find a good place to observe and see with your expanded eyes. See the blue light. It brings the ability to understand the truest truth of self and all that has been hidden.

Remember to look down to the base of the living tree. Notice the small world of the insects and bugs. They are ready to be acknowledged, as well. They are our great creators. They work with the hands of many, along with most every important system on earth, and they are no different by wanting to be acknowledged. Notice them by welcoming in the Small World for a while. Thank them and then do not go back to sleep, as they are part of the knowledge teams of Earth. Together they make up the whole of what keeps Earth sifting, growing, and producing. They help to feed us by preparing the soil, and they are essential.

Listen a moment to those that crawl upon the Earth as they wish to speak, too.

The snake, the lizard, crocodile and alligator, the gecko and the monitor lizard show up as totems. They show up just as the bear and the eagle show themselves to you. They declare that they are teachers and observers and make up a part of this ecosystem that wishes to be seen for the true knowledge that they hold.

I listen to my guides when I go to the forest. We all can slow down as the colors and textures envelope our senses and we get quiet listening for birds calling and the gentle rustle of the leaves in the wind. Ground as you walk beneath the trees. Open up to the still voice inside of you by quieting the mind. Listen to Nature all around and ask your guides of Nature to speak.

We are masters of blending in and becoming a perfect part of our home. Acknowledge your home now, be grateful for a moment. What do you love about where you live? What do you complain about? Imagine blending with your environment, so that every movement you make adds to the whole.

Listen, for we can teach you how to do this. It is a gentle reminder to be effective where you put your feet every day.

The Sasquatch of the great forests is called by many names. We are interdimensional travelers yet allow our physical bodies to sometimes be seen. We only wish to be within our family groups and do not leave much on a trail for humans to find, though some have seen us and know us for our sounds and smells.

We speak just as you do and are versed in healing tones and frequencies. We are a part of the healing of the area between Earth and Sky.

Our energetic field is strong and can be felt far away. We are Healers and Guides. ~ **The Sasquatch, Elder Brother**

The vibrancy of Fall can be felt within the body, so rest with this feeling of plenty. Acknowledge what you have learned this year about yourself. You have harvested much and this knowledge travels with you for the rest of your time on Earth and beyond.

Feel, sense and imagine that colder winds are coming. Lungfuls of cold air on a crisp, bright early morning. The sky will be the bluest it ever shows and enough dew, rain and snow to assist the Earth will fall for the next cycle. Bright berries on trees and pinecones and branches show up after the splendor of the Autumn leaves. Feel your body readying itself for the dark times that are coming when you will stay inside and count your blessings as you rest awhile.

Patience, practice, surrender and celebration! ~ **Curnunnos, Speaking about the Fall of the Year**

All can claim a sacred life. As the connection to Earth and Star is acknowledged and enlarged, we reflect the light and others sense this. No more are we separate. People now truly understand that we are one. ~ **White Flower, My Guide**

I hope that this book inspired you to look around for signs and symbols, and trust that you are connected to Source. We must learn to communicate with all of the realms, for they have much to teach us in the New World. Further generations depend on us learning to listen.

May you walk the middle road in freedom.

CHAPTER 14

Using the Codes

You have arrived at the point of understanding that good health can be gained by more measures than previously ever thought possible. The body and mind wish to partner with the whole of you. Take these codes and use them as a part of a happier and healthier life. ~ ***Nikola Tesla***

Boosting the Codes

Congratulations! You have made the decision to learn how to work with the next level of these Galactic and Angelic Healing and Regenerative Codes!

These light codes were implanted in my DNA during the time of Lemuria, which existed before and during the time of Atlantis. The transfer from teacher to student or client is held by Archangel Metatron, the Seraphim Angels, the Arcturians, and Ascended Master Kuthumi.

In this chapter, we introduce the next set of light codes and describe how they work when they are placed into the body of a human or animal.

In class, in person, or online, I describe how to release the codes from the body of the instructor into the student. It is a process that must be worked with over a two-day period. This process is called "the boost." A group of codes entering the body is called a "stream."

In order to work with the light codes, one must take the class, learn to use the codes, receive the transfer or boost and develop the frequency that is needed to use them over a two-day period. The transfer of the stream of codes is sacred and must be completed in class.

Healing in person or over distance or passing the codes to a student:

- Hold the frequency of love.

- Call in Creator and your Team of Light.

- Call in the four directions: the Golden Columns of Light, the Stargate, the Violet Flame, and the Blue Column of Light.

- Ground and clear yourself as well as the space you are working in.

- Call in the client or student and call in their Team of Light or have the student set their own intention.

- Intend to receive the visualization of the path and template.

- Walk on the path towards the template.

- Call in the Seven Galactic Suns, see the golden light shine down through our portal Sun, visualize the light pulsing down through you as the teacher and through the student or client, and down into the Earth where it continues until it aligns with the Inner Earth Sun at the core of the Earth.

- Return your consciousness to the template. See or imagine your bare feet on the color of the path that has come to you when you ask for the path and template.

- If you are using the codes to heal yourself or sending the codes by distance healing to a client, or boosting the codes into a student, view each code one by one and hold the image in your mind.

- Say the code's name out loud.

- Use the pendulum to ask if the code has transferred and if you need to, tap the code in more than once.

- If the code has transferred, go onto the next code.

- If you are passing the entire code stream to a student, view the codes one by one and hold each in your mind and say its name.

What to watch for during a healing:

- Changes in breathing

- Shifting the body

- Emotions

- Responses to questions

Some clients and students may feel nothing, they may notice changes later or feel emotional and physical changes right away. Everyone is different.

What to watch for when passing the Codes to a student:

- Changes in breathing

- Shifting the body

- Emotions

- Responses to questions

- How your body is feeling as the codes are being sent from you into the student

- The animation of the codes

Each code has a specific job, and each group has a specific focus.

The codes work in the following way:

Abundance

34. Abundance
35. Power Path
36. Masculine/Feminine Balance (Creativity/Self)
37. Heart/Mind Entrainment
38. Prosperity in the Tangible

Take Back Your Power

39. 5G Attenuation
40. Universal Lock and Key (Go Forward)
41. I Call My Power Back (Sacral Chakra)
42. Support Autonomic Nervous System (Safe, Rest, Digest)

Body, Mind and Emotions

43. Growth Stretch (Listening)
44. Higher Chakra Adjustment
45. I Am the Sun (Timed Healing)
46. Kaleidoscope Mind (Overwhelm Balance)
47. The Blue Column of Light (Clear Others from Your Field)

Clearing To Rise

48. Embodiment Prep (Mind and Emotions)
49. Release Judgement
50. The Godsphere (Clear Mind/Emotions, Stem Cell Encouragement)

Healing The Body

51. Archangel Michael's Rings of Light (Focused Healing)
52. Release Fear

Healing The Body cont.

53. Archangel Raphael's Copper Column of Light (Release Saboteur Weapons)
54. Resilience (Calm, Honor Self)
55. The Breath of The Soul I (Heart/Mind, Adds Value)

Advance

56. DNA/RNA (Expansion and Restructuring)
57. Flow Portal (Advance to The Next Step)
58. Glass Ceiling (Take the Final Step)

Balance

59. Walk the Middle Road (Go Forward in Peace)
60. Speed Up (Balance to Adjust Frequency)
61. Chaos (Pull Back into Your Own Power/Dragon DNA)

Angelic Expansion

62. Lift, Ignition
63. Draw (Pour Forth)
64. Spread Your Wings (Begin Next Step)

Settle and Open

65. The Codex (Akashic Records, Third Eye)
66. Release Inflammation
67. ADD/ADHD Support (Rest and Settle)
68. Support the Endocrine System (Settle Hormones)

The healing and regenerative codes can be combined with any other type of alternative or metaphysical modality. I use the codes every day on myself and send them out to clients in each reading and healing that I do.

The codes may be experienced as relaxing and even "nap producing." Remind your client or students to listen to their body and rest as their energy field adjusts to this healing. After several times of receiving the codes, the body adjusts past the need to nap, retains the relaxed feeling and will notice all of the rest of the positive results over time.

Congratulations! Thank you for going on this journey with me! This second book is a step into the future of healing and will in time evolve as new codes show themselves.

Abundance

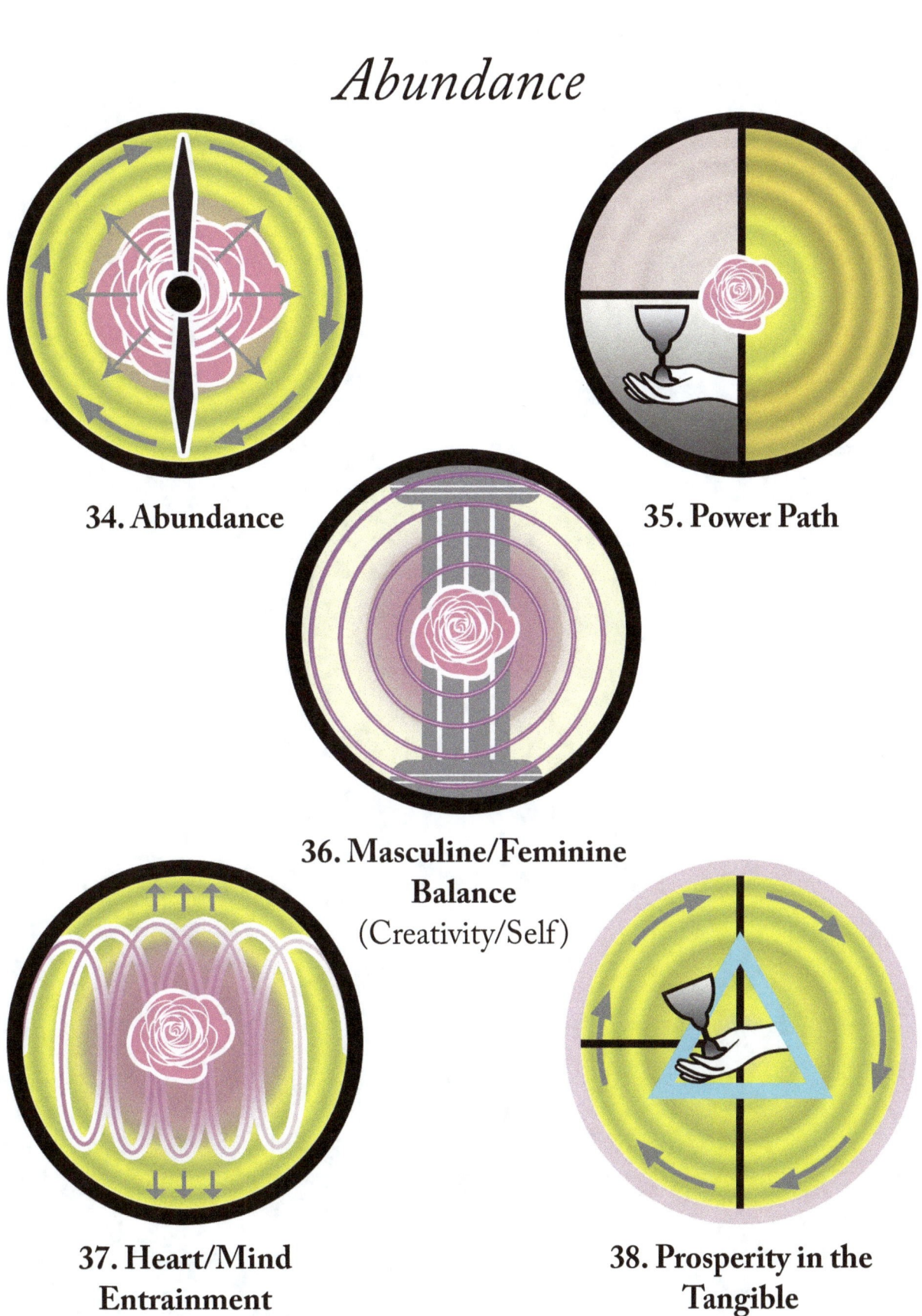

34. Abundance

35. Power Path

36. Masculine/Feminine Balance
(Creativity/Self)

37. Heart/Mind Entrainment

38. Prosperity in the Tangible

Take Back Your Power

39. 5G Attenuation

40. Universal Lock and Key
(Go Forward)

41. I Call My Power Back
(Sacral Chakra)

**42. Support Autonomic
Nervous System**
(Safe, Rest, Digest)

Body, Mind and Emotions

43. Growth Stretch
(Listening)

44. Higher Chakra Adjustment

45. I Am the Sun
(Timed Healing)

46. Kaleidoscope Mind
(Overwhelm Balance)

47. The Blue Column of Light
(Clear Others from Your Field)

Clearing To Rise

48. Embodiment Prep
(Mind and Emotions)

49. Release Judgement

50. The Godsphere
(Clear Mind/Emotions, Stem
Cell Encouragement)

Healing The Body

51. Archangel Michael's Rings of Light
(Focused Healing)

52. Release Fear

53. Archangel Raphael's Copper Column of Light
(Release Saboteur Weapons)

54. Resilience
(Calm, Honor Self)

55. The Breath of The Soul I
(Heart/Mind, Adds Value)

Advance

56. DNA/RNA
(Expansion and Restructuring)

57. Flow Portal
(Advance to The Next Step)

58. Glass Ceiling
(Take the Final Step)

Balance

59. Walk the Middle Road
(Go Forward in Peace)

60. Speed Up
(Balance to Adjust Frequency)

61. Chaos
(Pull Back into Your Own
Power/Dragon DNA)

Angelic Expansion

62. Lift, Ignition

63. Draw
(Pour Forth)

64. Spread Your Wings
(Begin Next Step)

Settle and Open

65. The Codex
(Akashic Records, Third Eye)

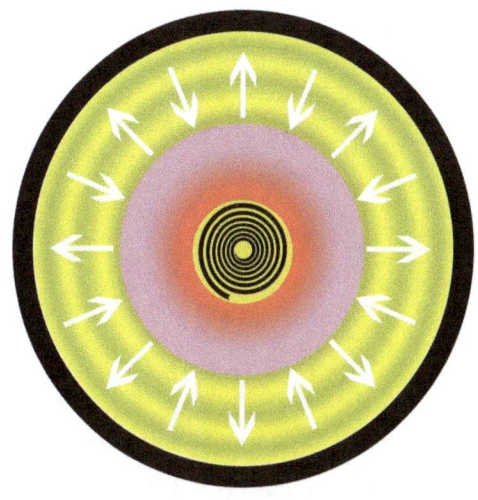

66. Release Inflammation

67. ADD/ADHD Support
(Rest and Settle)

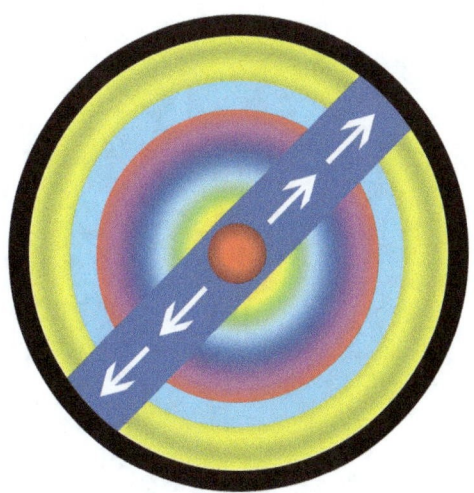

**68. Support the
Endocrine System**
(Settle Hormones)

Metaphysicians and Groups

Mari Beckman's website is *www.maribeckman.com* for classes, AOYE card deck, readings and merchandise.

Find **Todd Medina** and **Morgan Lee** on Soulogy and Soulogynetwork on Facebook, Instagram and many other platforms.

Find **Morgan Lee** at *www.zeropointing.com* for classes and readings.

Hands Of Light is a private support group on Facebook. We pray and send healing for those who reach out.

Sonia Jorgensen and **Spirit2Spirit** can be found on Facebook and Instagram
Spirit2Spirit offers personal healing to return to wholeness through the balance of body, mind and spirit. We partner with horses, Nature, and the community to aid us in this journey.

Jeffery Azanon St. Rose
Ascension Activations, Star Seed Oracle Card Deck and line of Sacred Geometry Pendants can be found on Facebook, Instagram and Etsy.
www.azanon.com

Nancy Rebecca
Blue Light Movement page can be found on Facebook
www.intuitivemind.org
Nancy has written many blogs about the blue light and has videos on Youtube on the subject.

Amaral Valle-Torres can be found on Facebook and at *Cristianamaralvalle@gmail.com* for Breathwork

Rev. Lola Singer
Light Language Artist and Singer
Usui Reiki Master, CHIOS Energy Master/Teacher
E-mail *lola@lightlanguagearts.com*
www.lolasinger.com

Derek Condit Intuitive/Clairvoyant, Energy Healer
Mystical Wares, 17869-State Route 536, Mount Vernon,WA 98273
Shungite Retaile: *www.mysticalwares.com*

Debora Stelfox, numerologist, love and relationship coach can be reached at *stelritz@foxinternet.net*

Deborah O'Connor
Quantum healing and regression with core trauma clearing and repatterning.
oconner.debbie1965@yahoo.com
503-333-1445

Patricia (Pat) Brack
Psychic, Spiritual Teacher, Energy Healer
patbrack9@gmail.com

Spain Adventures
www.SpainAdventures.com
844 41SPAIN

In Appreciation

Many thanks are given to those who supported the writing of this book and the work. They are listed in random order.

The Small Group, Steve Lee and all the shamans from around the country that supported us on our travels.

The Chiefs and Medicine Men and Women in spirit, especially Grandfather Rainbow, Medicine Man, Puyallup and Tulalip. Washington State, Lorraine Joseph, Puyallup Tribe Elder, Shaker Church healer and spiritual warrior, Washington State, Chief East Lee, Lakota, Eagle Butte, South Dakota and The Little Church in Tulalip, Washington.

Special gratitude to Lauri Wilson, my teacher. I remembered nothing and you guided me.

The Wheel: Barb, Melanie, Debbie, Amaral and especially Edi, our guide and teacher who showed us Spain in a way that made each one of us fall in love with it and the people of the country.

For a perfect place to write, I thank Monique and Les, Missy and Zac and Deb and Bruce.

The Ladder and my students and friends. Thank you for supporting the AOYE work, but mostly for allowing me to be your student, as I always learn from you. My Sunday classes are the highlight of my week. To my Mentorship Class, The Mentos, I thank you!

Hands of Light for good healing offered daily on Facebook and those of you who were part of early code trials.

Thank you to the Soulogy Network, Morgan Lee and Todd Medina, all of my radio friends, especially Gary Mantz and Suzanne Mitchell of KKNW, and the people who come to watch my podcast Metaphysical Meltdown.

Much gratitude to my dearest friends who worked with the codes as soon as they were birthed! Thank you for the trust, feedback and support.

My thanks to Pat Brack for being such a great teacher, channel and friend.

A special, grateful thank you to Melanie Long, space and time traveler.

So many thank you's to Deborah Stelfox, the Love Guru. She helped me when I was looking for a place to move. She told me to find a house that aligned with us numerologically. She helped me change my name when we got married. Thank you, Deborah, you are a beautiful heart of love!

Thank you to Doce Blant Publishing and Pat Brack, editor.

Our thanks go to Kathleen McCummings for all things Pennsylvania! And for looking out for us.

My deep loving thanks goes to Thom Beckman for transforming the codes off a piece of paper drawn badly by me and into art. Thank you for always being right next to me.

References

Cooper, D. & Crosswell, K. (2010, December). The keys to the universe: Access the ancient secrets by attuning to the power and wisdom of the cosmos. *Inner Traditions/Bear*.

Rebecca, N. (2023). Intuitive psychic development teacher. *YouTube*. https://www.youtube.com/@nancyrebecca

www.ingramcontent.com/pod-product-compliance
Lightning Source LLC
Chambersburg PA
CBHW080959120626
46546CB00010B/2960

* 9 7 8 1 9 5 5 4 1 3 2 5 1 *